EUGENE ONEGIN

EUGENE ONEGIN

Translated from the Russian of
ALEXANDER PUSHKIN

by DOROTHEA PRALL RADIN
and GEORGE Z. PATRICK

University of California Press
Berkeley · 1937

UNIVERSITY OF CALIFORNIA PRESS
BERKELEY, CALIFORNIA

———

CAMBRIDGE UNIVERSITY PRESS
LONDON, ENGLAND

COPYRIGHT, 1937, BY THE
REGENTS OF THE UNIVERSITY OF CALIFORNIA

CONTENTS

Introduction, page v

Eugene Onegin, page 1

Notes, page 215

ALEXANDER PUSHKIN
1799-1837

*From a painting by B. A. Tropinin.
The original is in the Tredyakov Gallery, Moscow.*

INTRODUCTION

ALEXANDER PUSHKIN was born in Moscow in 1799 and was killed in a duel in 1837. He is Russia's best-known poet. His aristocratic birth, his liberal principles, his four years of not very severe exile in South Russia, his leadership in Russian literary circles of his own day and his great service to the Russian language in giving it fluency and grace, together with the long list of his poems and his prose writings are facts easily to be found in English books. The *Encyclopaedia Britannica* gives him a page under "Pushkin," and his latest and most authoritative biography is that by Ernest J. Simmons soon to be published by Harvard University Press; readers who would compromise on length will find a brief but admirable estimate of his writings in Baring's *Outline of Russian Literature*. The Soviet Government holds Pushkin in such high esteem that it has just published a monumental work of 1179 pages, *The Literary Heritage of Pushkin*, part of a national plan for commemorating, in 1937, the hundredth anniversary of Pushkin's death.

Almost as obvious and undeniable as these facts is the statement that *Eugene Onegin*, a narrative poem in eight cantos, written intermittently between the years 1823 and 1831, is Pushkin's greatest work. And if not undenied or undeniable, it is still a literary commonplace among even the mildest students of the Russian novel that Tatyana, the heroine of the story, is the first shining picture in that long line of lovely and courageous Russian women whom Nekrasov, Turgenev, Dostoyevsky, and Tolstoy have helped to make one of the glories of nineteenth-century Russian literature.

This information being so well known or so easily ascertainable, all that is needed here is a few technical comments with respect to the present translation.

The degree of accuracy it may have attained is due entirely to Professor Patrick, who not only supplied a complete prose version which I have followed constantly, but who carefully corrected, also, many slips and misinterpretations.

As for previous translations, so far as I know there has been, until this year, only one complete translation in English, that by Lieutenant-Colonel Spalding, published in 1881 and now out of print. In late autumn, this year, a translation by Babette Deutsch appeared in a volume of Pushkin's prose and verse. There are French translations, and two excellent German ones: Bodenstedt's, and the recent translation of Theodor Commichau, edited with notes by Arthur Luther. I have made free use of Arthur Luther's notes and of Vaclav Lednicki's comments in Belmont's Polish translation of Onegin; I have also translated Pushkin's own notes where they seemed useful to English readers.

As for the Russian editions from which this translation is made, I have finally used Pushkin's own arrangement of the poem almost as he published it, and have added very few of the stanzas found and included only after his death. I have also omitted *Onegin's Journey*, which was originally published separately, and which I think weakens the poem.

Now, a few words in explanation of the meter and rhyme-form of the present version. Pushkin wrote the Russian in fourteen-line stanzas with eight or nine syllables to the line. The rhyme scheme is: a*b*a*b* c*c*dd e*ff*e gg, a feminine ending being indicated by italics. This stanza I have followed in English, except that in lines 1 and 3 I have dropped the rhyme but retained the feminine endings; in lines 5-14 I have kept the rhymes of the Russian but disregarded the distinction of masculine and feminine endings. This has not only allowed more freedom and so made it possible to come less far from Pushkin's characteristic flowing ease, but it has also avoided the effect of jingling which so many short and rhyming lines produce in English, an effect not so noticeable in Russian, where the like inflections of many words make the rhymes less emphatic. To help this lack of emphasis I have used many run-on lines and often slighted the rhymes, though without omitting them.

Pushkin's diction is as easy and unstrained as his versification, and I have therefore used fairly informal and contemporary English. But Pushkin wrote his poem in the early nineteenth century, when for a heroine to declare her love unasked to a hero was an act calling for great honesty and courage, so that in some passages I have thought slightly stilted phrases best suited to stilted conventions.

Professor Noyes, of the University of California, with whom I first read *Eugene Onegin* as a student, has given the whole translation the most generous and elaborate criticism, which has, I think, very considerably raised its tone. I am also indebted to Mr. Harold A. Small, Editor of the University of California Press, for his painstaking and valuable suggestions and corrections, and to my family and friends for help in words and phrasing.

D. P. R.

BERKELEY, CALIFORNIA,
    1936

Canto ONE

*And he is in haste to live and
in a wild hurry to feel.*

—PRINCE VYAZEMSKY.

1

"My uncle's life was always upright
And now that he has fallen ill
In earnest he makes one respect him:
He is a pattern for us still.
One really could not ask for more—
But heavens, what a fearful bore
To play the sick-nurse day and night
And never stir beyond his sight!
What petty, mean dissimulation
To entertain a man half dead,
To poke his pillows up in bed,
And carry in some vile potation,
While all the time one's thinking, 'Why
The devil take so long to die?'"

2

So mused a youthful scapegrace flying
Along the post road thick in dust,
The only heir of all his kindred,
By the decree of Jove the Just.
Friends of Lyudmila and Ruslan,
Let me bring forward this young man
As hero of my tale without
More preamble or roundabout.
My friend Eugene Onegin, then,
Was born beside the Neva; you
May have been born there, reader, too,
Or lived as glittering denizen.
I also used to sojourn there,
But now I dread the northern air.

3
His father served with great distinction
And lived along on credit. He
Would give his three balls every season
And so went bankrupt finally.
The fates were gentle with Eugene:
At first a French *Madame* had been
His guardian—then *Monsieur*. The child
Was lovable though somewhat wild.
Monsieur l'Abbé, the needy tutor,
Taught him his lessons half in jest
And treated morals lightly, lest
He should appear the persecutor.
The Summer Garden saw the pair
Come frequently to take the air.

4
Now when Eugene had reached the season
Of ardent youth when passion soars
Or tender longing fills the bosom,
Monsieur was driven out of doors.
Behold our hero!—not a flaw;
Modeled on fashion's latest law;
A London dandy, combed and curled,
Prepared at last to see the world.
His French was perfect; he could write
And speak without a foreign taint;
His bow was free of all constraint,
His step in the mazurka light.
The verdict was no more than truth:
A charming, cultivated youth.

5

We all achieve a little learning
Somehow, somewhere, with the result
That dazzling by one's erudition
With us is never difficult.
And so Eugene, by those who grudged
Their praises often, was adjudged
Well read—almost to pedantry.
He could discourse most happily
Like an inspired amateur
On anything in Christendom,
And when the talk grew grave, become
The wise and silent connoisseur,
Then suddenly let fly a shaft
Of wit, till all the ladies laughed.

6

Latin of late is out of fashion,
And so our scholar, if I am
To tell the truth, could muster barely
Enough to read an epigram,
To mention Juvenal, and, better,
To add a *Vale* to his letter,
Or quote from Virgil without break
Two lines, though not without mistake.
He had no love for history's pages
Nor any antiquarian lust
For digging into ancient dust,
But anecdotes of other ages
From Romulus to us he'd find
And store away within his mind.

7

Of poetry, that lofty mistress,
He was no votary devout
Nor knew an iamb from a trochee
However one might count them out.
Theocritus and Homer with
Their kind he damned, but Adam Smith
He read till he was a profound
Economist. He could expound
Wherein the wealth of nations lies
And what it lives on and how all
It needs is raw material,
Not gold. His father was less wise,
It seems, and could not understand
His son: he mortgaged all his land.

8

All the things Eugene had studied
I could not possibly impart,
But that wherein he was a genius,
Which was his own peculiar art,
That which from youth had been his pleasure,
The toil and torment of his leisure,
Which filled his days of idleness
With melancholy, vague distress—
That was the art which Ovid sung,
The art of love, to which he died
A martyr in Moldavia's wide
And barren wilderness, among
Barbarian tribes, no more to see
His own far-distant Italy.

9

The fire of love torments us early,
Chateaubriand has said. Indeed,
Nature is not our guide, but rather
The first salacious book we read.
Beholding love in some romance
We seek to know it in advance
Of our own season, and meanwhile
All other joys seem puerile.
Intent on this foretaste of bliss
We spoil it by our very haste,
Our youthful fervor goes to waste
And all our lives are lived amiss.
Such realizations came to vex
Eugene. But how he knew the sex!

10

How soon he learned to cloak his feelings,
To force his quarry to believe
Him true, to languish, dark and jealous,
To hide his hope—then undeceive;
To seem by turns subservient,
Proud, thoughtful, or indifferent,
With flaming eloquence to burn,
Or sit profoundly taciturn.
How in his notes of love unbounded
He threw discretion to the breeze,
Careless of all but how to please,
And how his glance, at once compounded
Of soft and keen, would then appear
To start with the obedient tear.

11
How skillfully he played the novice!
How well he knew the smiling ways
That startle an unpracticed maiden
And capture her with pleasant praise.
How he could seize the moment where,
Relenting at his feigned despair,
She yielded some half-meant caress
To his impassioned, shrewd address!
How ardently he then would sue
For an avowal! And at last,
When he perceived her heart beat fast,
Demand a secret rendezvous!
And then alone with her how he
Would tutor her in privacy!

12
How early he had learned to trouble
The heart of many a tried coquette;
And when he chose to crush his rivals,
What cunning pitfalls he could set!
With what malevolence he stung
Them with the poison of his tongue!
But you, you happy husbands, stayed
His friends: the married rake who made
A special point to pay him court,
Well versed in Faublas's strategy,
The old man prone to jealousy,
The cuckold with the pompous port,
Completely satisfied with life,
Himself, his dinner, and his wife.

13-14
How from some meek and modest widow
He could attract a pious glance
And enter into conversation
With bashful, blushing countenance!
How, trifling with some ladylove,
He could discourse upon the worth
Of Plato's doctrines and could move
A pretty simpleton to mirth!
So from the forest's inmost heart
The savage starving wolf will creep
Upon the fold—all are asleep
And helpless; swifter than a dart
The cruel thief has snatched his prey
And in a flash is far away.

15
They bring his letters in the morning
Before he's thought of getting dressed;
Three houses ask him for the evening,
Requesting him to be their guest.
A children's name-day feast, a ball,
Which shall he start with of them all?
No matter, he will manage it!
Meantime, in raiment exquisite,
And hatted à la Bolivar,
The picture of a youthful spark,
Eugene is driven to the Park
To saunter in the open air
Until his watch with pleasant chime
Announces it is dinnertime.

16

Then to a sledge. The dark has fallen,
And to the driver's loud "Make way!"
He's whirled along; his beaver collar
Grows white beneath the frosty spray.
So to Talon's, for he's aware
His friend Kaverin waits him there.
He enters, and the pleasant pop
Of corks arises, and the plop
Of gurgling wine. The roast beef vies
With truffles, youth's delight,—the queen
And flower of the French cuisine,—
And the far-famed Strassburg pies.
Then Limburg cheese, mature and old,
And pineapple, all yellow gold.

17

The thirst that comes from eating cutlets
Still calls for wine, but the ballet,
His watch announces to Onegin,
Already must be under way.
And so the caustic arbiter
Of greenrooms and the theater,
The somewhat fickle appanage
Of lovely ladies of the stage,
Is driven off to view the play.
The stormy audience huzza,
Ready to clap the *entrechat*
And hiss Racine and boo Corneille,
Or call Moïna back because
They love to hear their own applause.

18

O magic country! There Fonvizin,
The friend of freedom, satire's bold
Old master, and the imitative
Knyazhnin shone forth in days of old.
There young Semyonova bore off
The palm of praise with Ozerov,
The idols of their countrymen.
Katenin brought to life again
The stately genius of Corneille;
And Shakhovskoy's tumultuous rout
Of biting farces were brought out
And Didelot was crowned with bay.
And in the shadow of the wings
I dreamed youth's sweet imaginings.

19

Dear goddesses of mine! Where are you?
Hear my unhappy voice and say,
Have other maidens filled your places
To triumph where you once held sway?
And shall I hear you sing once more?
Shall I behold you sweep and soar,
The spirits of the Russian dance?
Or shall my melancholy glance
View faces in a world unknown,
Turning upon them as they pass
My disenchanted opera glass,
Gazing at mirth I have outgrown!
Then shall I yawn and silently
Regret my past felicity?

20

The house is full, the boxes glitter,
The pit is like a seething cup,
The gallery claps with loud impatience,
The curtain rustles—and goes up.
There, half of air and all aglow,
Obedient to the magic bow,
Circled by nymphs in lovely bands,
Istomina, resplendent, stands.
Balanced on one toe, tremulous,
She slowly whirls the other round,
Then with a sudden leap and bound
Flies as if blown by Aeolus.
She winds, unwinds and, light as feather,
In mid-air beats her feet together.

21

The house applauds. Onegin enters,
And, having trod on many a toe,
He studies through his opera glasses
The ladies whom he does not know.
His eye runs over every tier,
But gowns and faces all appear
To leave him far from satisfied.
He bows to men on every side,
Then carelessly begins to view
The stage and what is going on,
Averts his face and starts to yawn,
And mutters, "Time for something new!
The ballet pleased me once, but how
Didelot himself does bore me now!"

22
But still the cupids, snakes, and devils
Career about and scream and roar;
The tired lackeys in their sheepskins
Still doze before the entrance door;
And still they stamp and hiss and rap,
Or blow their noses, cough, and clap,
And still, outside and in, the night
Is all ablaze with lantern light.
The coach horse paws the ground or stands
Half frozen by the tedious wait,
And round the fires the cabbies rate
Their masters as they warm their hands;
But our Eugene, as you may guess,
Has long since left to change his dress.

23
Shall I depict in faithful colors
The private room where the mundane
Disciple of exacting fashion
Was dressed, undressed, and dressed again?
Everything London's nicest taste
Exports across the Baltic waste
To get, for gewgaws smart or strange,
Timber and tallow in exchange,
All that the workshop and the loom
Of greedy Paris could produce
Of luxuries as an excuse
For useful barter, in the room
Of our philosopher were seen—
The seer and sage just turned eighteen.

24

Pipes from Stamboul with stems of amber,
Bronzes and porcelain *en masse*,
And, that enjoyment of the pampered,
Perfumes in flagons of cut glass.
Steel files and combs elaborate
And scissors curved and scissors straight,
Brushes with thirty-odd details,
Some for the teeth, some for the nails.
(Rousseau could never understand,
They tell us, how the worthy Grimm
Could clean his nails in front of him,
The visionary firebrand:
The champion of natural rights
Here hardly followed his own lights.)

25

A man may see his nails are polished,
Yet be a useful citizen;
Why quarrel with one's generation?
Custom's a despot among men.
At any rate in our Eugene
A new Kaverin now was seen,
A dandy envied, watched, and thus
Forced to be most meticulous.
So when at last he sallied forth
After three hours before the glass,—
For so three hours at least would pass,—
'Twas like a Venus come to earth
Who thus in flighty mood essayed
The rôle of man in masquerade.

[14]

26
Now that I've drawn your kind attention
To fashion and the mode, you may
Expect me to describe more fully
My hero's elegant array;
A somewhat trying task, I fear,
Although description is my sphere,
For *pantaloons*, *frock coat*, and *vest*
No Russian wording can suggest,
And even now you must behold
How I have patched my halting style
With words of foreign domicile
Too lavishly. And yet of old,
To freshen my vocabulary,
I searched the Academy Dictionary.

27
But that is not the point at present:
Let's rather hurry to the ball
Where headlong in his cab Onegin
Has dashed already. On past tall
Dim houses where the horses' feet
Make echoes in the sleeping street
The carriage lamps, a double row,
Cast rainbow shadows on the snow.
Sown all around with firepots
A great house gleams; across the glass
Of lighted windows shadows pass,
Profiles of heads, and groups and knots
Of ladies with their cavaliers—
One moment, then each disappears.

28

Up drives our hero. Past the doorman
He darts and up the marble stair
Swift as an arrow; with one gesture
He brushes back a lock of hair—
And enters. Everywhere a crowd:
The orchestra is playing loud
And a mazurka fills the floor
While all about is crush and roar.
The spurs of many a guardsman clash
And tiny feet go flying by
And many a captivated eye
Flies after them. Then while the crash
Of violins drowns out the sound
A jealous whispering goes round.

29

In my gay days of youthful passion
Balls were my mad delight. Then, too,
No better spot for an avowal
Or for delivering *billets-doux*.
You married folk, discreet and nice,
I offer you some sound advice:
(I beg you, note my words with care)
For I would caution you, Beware!
And you, Mammas, had better bend
A stricter glance on those coquettes
Your daughters. Up with your lorgnettes!
For otherwise—Ah, Heaven forfend!
These secrets I instruct you in,
Since I myself long ceased to sin.

30

Alas! In my pursuit of pleasure
How many years have slipped away!
Yet were my morals not to suffer
I still should dote on balls today.
I love mad youth; I love the crowd,
Glitter and joy without a cloud,
The dresses, exquisite, complete,
And I adore the ladies' feet!
But you will hardly find, all told,
Six pretty feet in Russia. Yet
Two tiny feet I can't forget,
Although I've grown so sad and cold.
Their memory will not depart
And still in dreams they stir my heart.

31

Ah, little feet! To me, the madman,
What desert land will fail to bring
A vision of you! In what country
Do you now tread the flowers of spring?
Bred in the softness of the East,
Our sullen northern snow long ceased
To hold your imprint. You were such
As loved the soft luxurious touch
Of silky rugs— And are they past,
Those days when in you I forgot
Glory and country and my lot
As exile? Yes, they could not last,
And no more trace of them is seen
Than of your footfalls on the green.

32

Diana's breast, the cheeks of Flora,
Are no doubt charming. But to me
Far lovelier and more enthralling
The fair feet of Terpsichore!
They promise us they will afford
An incomputable reward
And with their beauty light the fire
Of uncontrollable desire.
Elvina! I commemorate
Your feet! at all times: half concealed
Beneath the table; on the field
Of spring; in winter by the grate;
Upon the polished parquet floor;
On granite rocks along the shore!

33

I can recall a stormy seashore:
The waves came rushing one above
Another in a fury, only
To lie before her feet in love.
I would have found it ah! how sweet,
As did the waves, to kiss her feet.
For never in my maddest days
When all my youth was yet ablaze
Did I so wildly long to press
The lips of Armida, or burn
To kiss her rosy cheeks or yearn
To touch her breast with a caress.
No, such a transport as then tore
My heart I never felt before.

34

And I remember one more picture—
In secret dreams again I stand
Holding for her the happy stirrup,
Her little foot within my hand.
Once more my fancy burns, once more
Her touch seems suddenly to pour
New streams of lifeblood through my heart,
Once more with love and pain I smart.
But sing no more, my noisy lyre,
These haughty damsels of the earth,
Enchantresses who are not worth
The love and songs that they inspire.
Their speeches and their glances cheat
As often as their little feet.

35

And our Onegin? He abandons
The ball for bed, half overcome
With sleep, as Petersburg the tireless
Is wakened by the noisy drum.
The cabman trudges to his stand,
Merchant and peddler are at hand,
An Ochta milkgirl hurries by,
The hard snow crunching frostily.
It is the pleasant morning stir:
The shutters open, in blue curls
The smoke from many a chimney whirls,
And, careful German manager,
The baker in his paper cap
Has answered many an early rap.

36

But wearied of the evening's turmoil,
Turning the morning into night,
The child of luxury and pleasure
Sleeps softly in the shaded light.
Then well past midday he awakes
To lead again, till morning breaks,
His life monotonous though gay,
Tomorrow like its yesterday.
But in this round of daily bliss
Was my Eugene quite satisfied?
To the proud victor in the pride
Of youth did nothing seem amiss?
In spite of all did he remain
At feasts and fêtes unspoiled and sane?

37

No, he had lost his freshness early
And wearied of society.
Beauties and belles no longer caused him
A stronger passion than ennui.
He took no pleasure in intrigue,
His friendships only brought fatigue;
He could not sit the livelong day
Drinking champagne to wash away
The rare beefsteak and Strassburg pie;
Nor could he be prepared to make
Bright sallies with a bad headache;
And though a hothead, finally
He found his interest weakening
In pistols, swords, and dueling.

38

A sickness,—for its cure and treatment
We ought to find the formula,—
The thing they call the spleen in England,
Our Russian hypochondria,
Had mastered him by slow degrees;
And though, thank God, it did not please
The youth to blow his brains out, still
Life was a desert, dark and chill.
So, like Childe Harold, steeped in gloom,
Oblivious to the allure
Of gossip, boston, sighs demure,
He would pass through a drawing room
Observing nothing that was there,
Nor altering his cheerless air.

42*

Fine ladies of the world of fashion,
You he abandoned first of all,
For at our age your upper circles
Undoubtedly begin to pall.
And though perhaps some lady may
Discourse on Bentham and on Say,
Their conversation as a rule
Is innocent but tedious drool.
Besides, they are so virtuous,
So lofty-minded and so clever,
So full of pious, pure endeavor,
So circumspect, so scrupulous,
So inaccessible of mien,
Their very sight brings on the spleen.

---

* Stanzas 39, 40, and 41 are not in the Russian text.

43
And you, young beauties of the evening,
Whom the wild droshkies dash along
The streets of Petersburg at midnight,
Eugene has left your boisterous throng.
Refusing all his visitors,
He had immured himself indoors
And shunned all riotous delight.
Yawning, he seized his pen to write—
But any stubborn work instilled
Disgust in him; no line would flow
From off his wavering pen, and so
He did not join that vexing guild
Of scribblers on whom I may pass
No judgment, being of their class.

44
Once more a prey to doing nothing,
His spirit sick with futile rage,
He sat down with the worthy purpose
Of mastering wisdom's heritage.
He filled a shelf with books and read—
But all to no avail. Instead,
One was a bore, one, mad pretense,
No conscience here, and there no sense;
Stale judgments everywhere he looks,
The old too old, the new all cast
In the old forms, and so at last,
Like women, he abandoned books,
And covered with a mourning-veil
The shelf of wisdom dead and stale.

45

Now I had likewise left the turmoil
And thrown convention's yoke aside,
And at this time we formed our friendship.
His traits and temper satisfied
My liking, the unique degree
To which he raised his oddity,
His dreams, his wit, that struck so close.
I was malicious, he morose.
We both had suffered passion's play
And we were weary of our parts,
The fire had died out in our hearts,
Though barely started on life's way,
And from blind fortune or from men
We hoped for nothing good again.

46

He who has lived and thought can hardly
Do otherwise than scorn his race;
He who has ever felt is troubled
With dreams of that which once took place.
No magic moments now will cause
Delight, the worm of memory gnaws
His heart and brings him vain regret;
But still it often does beget
A certain charm in conversation.
At first Onegin's sharp retorts
Put me a little out of sorts,
But later I felt no vexation
At his half-bilious sallies and
The sarcasm at his command.

47

How often in the summer evenings
When the night sky hung clear and bright
Above the waters of the Neva
Where yet there shone no mirrored light
From fair Diana's countenance,
We dreamed again of young romance
And thought of early love, again
Carefree and fond as we were then.
And the night air, so pure and good,
Without a word we breathed in deep;
Till like the prisoner whom sleep
Bears from his cell to some green wood,
Our reveries and musings bore
Us back to days of youth once more.

48

Eugene would stand in silence, leaning
Against the granite parapet,
Just as the poet did, he tells us,
Lost in old longing and regret.
No sound except a distant shout
When watchmen called the hours out
Or suddenly the rush and beat
Of cabs along a far-off street.
A lonely boat swept down the stream
And with the splash of oars were borne
A wild song and a fainter horn,
And we were spellbound in a dream.
But sweeter still than this delight
Are Tasso's octaves on the night.

49

O blue waves of the Adriatic,
O Brenta, river of my choice,
I yet shall look on you in rapture,
I yet shall hear your magic voice,
Sacred to all Apollo's sons
And known to me through Albion's
Proud lyre and ever dear to me.
The nights of golden Italy
I shall delight in to my fill!
Then in a dark mysterious boat
Some Venice maid with me will float
And now speak softly, now be still.
And she shall teach to me the tongue
Of Petrarch in which love is sung.

50

Oh, will it come, my hour of freedom?
For it is time to hear my cry.
I wait fair winds upon the seashore
And hail the vessels sailing by.
When shall I start my own free course?
When, under storm clouds, shall I force
My way across the battling sea
And leave a land so harsh to me?
And when at last I leave it, then
By the warm seas beneath the sky
Of sunny Africa I'll sigh
For gloomy Russia once again,
Where I had learned to love and weep
And where my heart lies buried deep.

51

Onegin was about to travel
With me in foreign countries when
Fate cut the tie that bound our fortunes;
For years we did not meet again.
His father died. The creditors
Gathered before Onegin's doors
In greedy crowds, and each one came
Prepared to justify his claim.
Eugene, who hated legal traps
And law courts, took what came from chance,
Renouncing his inheritance
As no great forfeit. Or perhaps
Some vague presentiment, some breath
Spoke of his uncle's coming death.

52

And then a letter from the bailiff
Came suddenly, to notify
Him that his uncle now lay dying
And wished to bid his heir goodbye.
Eugene no sooner read the news
Than he was off, prepared to use
What speed he could along the way,
But yawning as he thought what lay
Ahead— what tedious hours he'd spend
Before he was a moneyed man.
(And at this point my tale began.)
But when he reached his journey's end
He found the body laid in state
And finished with its earthly fate.

53

The courtyard swarmed with neighbors'
    servants:
From north and south, from west and east,
The dead man's friends and foes had
    gathered,
All lovers of a funeral feast.
They buried him, and priest and guest
Refreshed themselves. Then, as if pressed
By weighty business matters, they
Took solemn leave and went away.
Behold Eugene, a country squire,
Owner of factory and river,
Of wood and field! The spendthrift liver
Of yesterday was all afire
To lead a life of order here
And end his former free career.

54

Two days the new enchantment lasted:
The fields with their deserted look,
The coolness of the shady forest,
The quiet murmuring of the brook.
But on the third, field, wood, and hill
No longer caused his heart to thrill
And later sent him fast asleep,
So that he could no longer keep
The knowledge from himself: he knew
That though here were no palace halls,
No cards, no verses, and no balls,
The spleen dwelt in the country, too,
And would attend him all his life
Like one's own shadow or one's wife.

55

Now, I was born for country quiet,
To be some peaceful villager,
For there my lyre's note grows louder,
My dreams and fancies livelier.
There, consecrated to the sway
Of *far niente*, every day
I wander round the lonely lake
And every morning I awake
To leisure, sweet and innocent.
I seldom read, but sleep, nor aim
To capture swiftly flying fame.
Was it not so my past was spent?
And then, obscure, unknown to praise,
Did I not live my happiest days?

56

A country house upon its acres,
Love, flowers, and utter idleness—
I love them all, unlike Onegin.
Indeed, I'm always glad to stress
The great dissimilarity
Between my friend Eugene and me,
So that no mocking reader nor
Malicious-tongued inquisitor,
Searching a likeness out, may sniff
And shamelessly asseverate
I've drawn myself upon the slate,
Like Byron in his pride. As if
No artist ever had been known
To paint a portrait not his own!

57

All poets, let me say, are dreamers,
The friends of love. And so of old
Sweet phantoms visited me sleeping
Whose images my heart would hold
Long after, till the Muse had brought
Life to these secret forms of thought.
Indifferently I have sung
An ideal mountain maid or young
Girl slave upon the Salhir's shore.
But you, my friends, keep asking me:
"Which of these jealous maids is she
Whom in your verses you adore?
Who is the loved one to inspire
The song that rises from your lyre?

58

"Whose glance has fired your inspiration?
Whose sweet caress was adequate
Reward for all your pensive music?
Whom do your verses celebrate?"
No one, my friends, no one, God knows.
The pangs of love, its senseless throes,
I suffered without recompense.
Happy the man who can condense
The heat of love to poetry!
So, following in Petrarch's ways,
His heart's hot torment he allays
And yet augments his ecstasy.
He tastes of glory and its fruit—
But love has always made me mute.

59

Only when stormy love was over
Did my Muse enter. Then I found
My mind made free to seek the union
Between my dreams and magic sound.
I write, and my sad heart is eased,
My wandering pen no longer pleased
At each unfinished line to trace
Some tiny foot, some charming face.
The fire that was is burned to coal;
Now I, though sad, no longer weep,
And soon the storm will go to sleep
Forever in my quiet soul.
Then I may well begin a song
Some five-and-twenty cantos long.

60

Already I have planned my story
And named the hero, and meantime
I see that of my present novel
One chapter has been turned to rhyme.
I've looked it over carefully.
The contradictions that I see
I shall not alter now, but let
The censorship collect its debt.
And to the critics with my thanks
I send you, to be torn apart,
Newborn creation of my heart!
There on the Neva's well-known banks
To earn the tribute paid to fame:
Envy, abuse, and noisy blame.

Canto TWO

O rus.   O Rus!
—HORACE.

1

The place in which Onegin languished
Was a delightful country spot
Where lovers made for simpler pleasures
Would have been grateful for their lot.
The manor house itself was set
Apart beside a rivulet,
Cut off by hills from every storm.
Before it, flowery, golden-warm,
Meadows and cornfields stretched away,
And cattle cropped the grassy land,
And hamlets shone; while near at hand
The great neglected gardens lay
Where wistful dryads came and made
Their refuge in the deep green shade.

2

The ancient and time-honored mansion
Was built, as mansions ought to be,
According to the bygone liking
For sober, wise solidity.
High-ceilinged chambers everywhere,
Silk tapestry on couch and chair,
Ancestral portraits in a style
Outworn, and stoves of colored tile.
To us all this seems antiquated,—
I can't say why,—but then, our friend
Most probably did not descend
To notice that they were outdated;
For fashion or antiquity
Produced in him the same ennui.

3
So in the room where the old landlord
Had forty years of exercise
In bickering with his woman servant
Or staring out and catching flies
Eugene took up his domicile.
No inkstain there that might defile
The plainness of the oaken floor:
Two cupboards, sofa, desk—no more.
Behind one cupboard door a great
Account book lay and close at hand
Bottles and jugs of cider and
A calendar of 1808.
Onegin's uncle would not look
At any other kind of book.

4
Alone on his ancestral acres,
Hard put to it for any scheme
To pass the time, Eugene decided
To introduce a new régime.
Here in the wilds the sage recluse
Declared forced labor an abuse
And changed it for a light quitrent.
His serfs thanked fate and were content.
Not so the neighboring landlords; some
Smiled mockingly, while others found
These innovations going round
Unsafe, and looked extremely glum.
But on one point they all were clear:
Eugene was dangerous and queer.

5
At first, indeed, they came to visit,
But presently, when they had found
He usually had his stallion
Led out and saddled and brought round
To the back porch, when he should hear
Their family coaches drawing near—
Affronted by such insolence,
They one and all took deep offense.
"Our neighbor's just a firebrand,
A freemason, a boor. They say
He sits and drinks red wine all day.
He will not kiss a lady's hand.
He won't say 'Sir,' just 'Yes' and 'No.'"
Their view of him was very low.

6
Just then another country squire
Had come to live on his estate
Who caused the same amount of gossip
And called forth censure just as great.
Vladimir Lensky was his name.
Direct from Göttingen he came,
A poet and a devotee
Of Kant. From misty Germany
He brought complete enlightenment:
High dreams of freedom democratic,
A spirit ardent if erratic,
A tongue forever eloquent.
A handsome youth, with fire and grace,
And black curls falling round his face.

7

Unblighted by the world's corruption
And by its cold perfidiousness,
His soul was set on fire by friendship
Or by a maiden's soft caress.
He was a charming innocent
In matters of the heart, intent
Upon the glamour and the noise
Of this new world of untried joys
Which hope held up to view. He lulled
His doubts with dreams. But still for him
The aim of life was strange and dim,
A riddle over which he mulled
And struggled, eager to divine
The miracle of its design.

8

He thought somewhere some kindred spirit
Was born for union with his own,
Some maiden waiting for him hourly
And longing to be his alone.
He thought the men he loved would spend
Their lives in prison to defend
His honor, and would not demur
To crush his venomous slanderer.
He thought there were some men appointed
By fate whose lot it was to be
A sort of friendly hierarchy,
A deathless band of the anointed,
Whose light would pierce our dark abyss
Some day and lead the world to bliss.

9

Pity and generous indignation,
A passion for the common good,
The torment caused by love of glory,
All worked together in his blood.
And so he wandered, lyre in hand,
His heart exalted, through the land
Where Goethe and where Schiller sung,
In air where still their genius clung.
Nor did he shame the lofty arts
Protected by the sacred Nine;
His songs endeavored to enshrine
The noblest feelings of our hearts:
A maiden's dream of ecstasy,
The charm of grave simplicity.

10

The slave of love, he sang its praises
In stanzas like a limpid stream,
As simple as a maiden's fancies,
As artless as a childhood dream,
Clear as the moon in desert skies
That listens to a lover's sighs.
He sang of parting and of sorrow,
Of what-not and the misty morrow
And of the roses of romance.
He sang of countries far away
Where, weeping hotly, once he lay
Pillowed on silence' broad expanse.
He sang life's flowers dead and sere:
He then was in his eighteenth year.

11

Eugene alone could rightly value
Such talents in this arid waste,
And Lensky found the neighbors' dinners
Completely foreign to his taste.
He shunned their noisy conversations
About their dogs and their relations.
Indeed their sober talk of wine
And crops, though shrewd and genuine,
Did not exactly blaze with wit;
Nor was there any poet's fire
Nor brilliancy nor keen desire
Nor art nor social grace in it.
And certainly the ladies' words
Were quite as dull as were their lords'.

12

Both rich and personable, Lensky
Was thought an enviable match
And everyone who had a daughter—
Such was the custom—planned a match
With this half-Russian neighbor. They
Would manage, when he called, to say
How sad a single life must be
And ask the bachelor to tea
With Dunya at the samovar
To do the honors for their guest.
They'd whisper, "Dunya, do your best,"
And then they'd bring her her guitar,
And she would pipe as she was told,
Poor child, "Come to my halls of gold."

13
But Lensky had no inclination
For dalliance, it must be confessed;
While on the other hand Onegin
Aroused his deepest interest.
They met; and prose and poetry,
Cold ice and flame, firm rock and sea,
Were not so wholly different.
Quite bored at first, they underwent
A change of feeling to a state
Of liking in a certain way.
They met on horseback every day
And finally grew intimate.
So idleness achieved its end:
Each was the other's bosom friend.

14
But even such friendships are discarded
As prejudices of the past.
We rate ourselves alone as digits,
All others ciphers, to be classed
As vile by us, Napoleons
Among a million lesser ones
Created only for our tools,
And men of feeling we think fools.
Eugene was more forbearing. Though
Of course he knew and scorned mankind
As something very dull and blind,
All rules have their exceptions, so
Though alien to his intellect
He treated feeling with respect.

15

He listened with a smile to Lensky;
His bright and ardent conversation,
His unripe reasoning, and always
The poet's glance of inspiration,—
All this was novel to Eugene.
He struggled not to intervene
And chill such youthful ecstasy,
Thinking: "It is too bad of me
When bliss endures so short a space
To cloud this moment with regret.
His time will come; but meanwhile let
Him think the world a perfect place.
We must set down to youth's extremes
His youthful fire, his youthful dreams."

16

Between them everything was subject
For controversy and debate.
The treaty rights of ancient tribesmen,
Prejudices of antique date,
The fruits of learning, good and ill,
And life and fortune versatile,
And death, the mystery of ages,
Hung on the utterance of these sages.
Then, in the heat of argument,
Would Lensky eagerly rehearse
Fragments of northern poets' verse,
And our Eugene, the lenient,
Though missing an enormous deal
Would listen to his youthful zeal.

17

But oftener the tender passions
Engaged our youthful hermits' minds.
Onegin, freed from their dominion,
Discoursed of them as one who finds
Himself regretting quietly
The former tumult. Happy he
Who has outlived it. Happier still
The man who never felt that thrill,
Who conquered love by separation,
Hatred by lies—and yawned through life,
Bored by his friends and by his wife,
Untouched by jealous perturbation,
And never risked the ancestral hoard
Upon the treacherous gaming board.

18

When we enroll beneath the standard
Of safe and wise tranquillity,
And when love's passions are extinguished
And our wild whims and ecstasy
With their belated echoes seem
A foolish and outgrown extreme—
Then we, delivered from our spell,
May like to hear a stranger tell
His passionate and frenzied story
And feel our pulses stir again.
Just so some ancient veteran
Alone and shorn of former glory
Still loves to hear the young hussars
Recount their exploits in the wars.

19

And ardent youth is not secretive,
But always ready to impart
The love and hate, the joy and sorrow
Which animate its inmost heart.
Eugene, whose pride it was to be
The veteran lover, solemnly
Attended while his friend laid bare
His simple, fervent love affair,
Delighting in the utterance
Which artlessly disclosed his heart.
Thus without effort on his part
Onegin learned the youth's romance,
A tale of feeling it is true,
But long since anything but new.

20

He was indeed the sort of lover
Whose like we do not find today;
Only the mad soul of a poet
Is born to love in such a way.
At every time, in every place,
One single dream, one single face,
And one familiar sorrow still.
And neither distance bleak and chill,
Nor all the years of separation
Nor hours devoted to the arts
Nor lovely girls of foreign parts
Nor books nor scenes of animation
Could moderate his heart's desire
Still burning with its virgin fire.

21

Bewitched when still a boy by Olga,
Before he knew love's burning flames,
He used to watch the little maiden
With gentle pleasure at her games,
And in the shady wood he played
Alone with her. Their fathers made
Betrothal plans without demur,
Old friends and neighbors as they were.
Here in her peaceful country home
Beneath her parents' eyes she grew
As lilies of the valley do
That come at last to hidden bloom
Unnoticed in the clustering grass
By bees and butterflies that pass.

22

She gave the poet that first rapture
So poignant and so absolute.
Her image was the inspiration
Which first aroused his silent flute.
Farewell, you golden games of childhood,
For now he loved the deep-grown wildwood,
Silence and solitude and night,
The stars in heaven, the pale moon's light.
O Moon, the lamp of heaven! How
We used to walk in lonely grief
Until our tears would bring relief,
And vow the night to you— and now
You're but a makeshift, none too good,
For street-lamps in the neighborhood.

23

Olga was always good and modest,
Gay as the morning sun above,
As simple-hearted as the poet,
Sweet as the kiss of one's true love.
Her smile, her flaxen curls, her eyes
As blue as are the summer skies,
Her voice, her slimness, and her quick
And graceful movements—all.— But pick
Up any novel, you will see
Her portrait; it is charming, too,
And once it thrilled me through and through;
But now it bores me utterly.
Her elder sister, in her turn,
Is now, dear reader, our concern.

24

Her sister had been called Tatyana—
We are the earliest to proclaim
Deliberately in a novel
A heroine by such a name.
Why not? It has a pleasant ring
Although, I know, around it cling
The odors of the servants' hall
Or of antiquity. We all
Must grant the names in poorest taste
With us have greatest currency
(I am not counting poetry):
Our education is a waste
From which we learn to set great store
On affectation—nothing more.

25

Her sister, then, was named Tatyana,
We've said, and she did not possess
The charm of Olga's rosy freshness
Nor of her winning prettiness.
Somber and silent and withdrawn,
As timid as a woodland fawn,
Even in her own family
She seemed some stranger child. For she
Had never learned the childish art
Of blandishment, so sure a way
To please one's parents. And for play
She never seemed to have the heart;
But often sat alone and still
All day beside the window sill.

26

She was a friend to meditation
And always had been so; the stream
Of quiet country days she colored
With the bright fancies of her dream.
Her tender fingers never held
A needle while the blossoms swelled
In silken fullness and became
A pattern on the embroidery frame.
It is a sign of love of power
Which little girls who like to play
With an obedient doll betray
When decorously by the hour
They solemnly repeat to it
Their mother's lessons, bit by bit.

27

But from her very little-girlhood
Tatyana never had been known
To touch a doll or tell it gossip
Or what the fashion was in town.
And childish naughtiness was quite
As strange to her; but when at night
In winter darkness they would start
Old grisly tales, it thrilled her heart.
And when the nursemaid would collect
All Olga's friends from round about
Upon the grass to run and shout
With laughter hearty and unchecked,
Tatyana never joined their game—
It seemed so boisterous yet so tame.

28

She loved to stand before the sunrise
Upon the balcony and watch
The galaxy of stars departing
From the pale sky, and the first blotch
Of faintest light where earth met sky,
And feel the little winds that sigh
In greeting to the risen dawn.
And long before the dark had gone
In winter or the shadows ceased
To lie on half the world, while still
The quiet moon, remote and chill,
Shone dimly on the lazy east,
This hour was still her favorite
And she got up by candlelight.

29

She took to novel-reading early,
And all her days became a glow
Of rapturous love for the creations
Of Richardson and of Rousseau.
Her father, who was good and kind,
Had long ago been left behind
By modern ways, but in the main,
Although he thought books light and vain,
He did not think them any harm.
And when a man has never read,
The books his daughter takes to bed
With her will cause him no alarm.
As for his wife, there was no one
So much in love with Richardson.

30

She worshiped Richardson not only
Because she read so much of him;
Nor because Lovelace suited better
Than Grandison her girlish whim.
But in old days Princess Aline,
Her Moscow cousin there, had been
His satellite. Then she was still
A girl, engaged against her will
To him she later married, though
She sighed for one—unseen, unheard—
Whose mind and heart she much preferred.
Her Grandison was quite a beau,
A zealous devotee of cards,
And a young sergeant in the Guards.

31

Like his, her dress was always modish
And always most appropriate;
But, without asking her opinion,
They named the maiden's wedding date.
Her husband, in the wise belief
That he might thus divert her grief,
Moved to his country place where she
With God knows whom for company
Gave way to grief and was quite bent
On a divorce—then seemed to find
Her household duties claim her mind,
Grew used to things, and then content.
For heaven-sent habit soothes distress
And takes the place of happiness.

32

So habit quieted a sorrow
Which nothing else could have allayed,
And soon her cure was quite completed
By a discovery she made.
In days now empty and now full
She learned the trick of how to rule
Her husband like an autocrat,
And all went smoothly after that.
She watched the field-work under way,
She salted mushrooms for the next
Long winter, beat her maids when vexed,
And took the baths on Saturday,
Kept books, sent off the new recruits—
All without marital disputes.

33

She had been wont to write in albums
Of girlish friends in blood, and call
Praskovya her Pauline, and lengthen
Each sentence to a genteel drawl.
She laced her corsets very tight
And said her Russian *n*'s in quite
The best French manner, through her nose.
But by degrees she dropped her pose:
Corsets and album and Pauline,
The notebook full of tender rhyme—
All were forgotten, and in time
Akulka had replaced Céline;
Till finally she went about
In cap and wrapper wadded out.

34

Her husband loved his wife sincerely
And never gave her cause to frown,
But spent his days, serene and trustful,
Attired in a dressing gown.
So life rolled placidly along:
Sometimes at night a little throng
Of friendly neighbors would arrive,
All intimates, and all alive
With gossip or with sympathy;
And they would laugh and chat and smile
And time would pass unnoticed, while
Olga was bid to make the tea.
Supper, the end of one more day—
And then the guests would drive away.

35

In this calm life, the good old customs
Were laws from which they never swerved;
When Shrovetide came and merrymaking,
Then Russian pancakes must be served.
They made confession twice a year;
They held a carrousel as dear
As bowl-songs and the circle-dance.
And when with yawning countenance
The peasants listened to the mass
On Trinity, they'd drop a tear
Upon a sprig of lovage; air
Was not more needful than was kvass;
And guests at dinner ate and drank
In strict accordance with their rank.

36

And so they lived for years together
Till for the husband, old and hoary,
Death drew aside the final curtain
And he received his crown of glory.
One afternoon he left this life,
Mourned by his children and his wife,
The neighborhood, and all his clan,
More truly than is many a man.
A simple squire without caprice,
Kindly to all—and on the stone
That marks his grave these verses run.
A HUMBLE SINNER, NOW AT PEACE,
GOD'S SERVANT AND A BRIGADIER,
'TIS DMITRI LARIN SLEEPETH HERE.

37

When he returned to his Penates,
Vladimir Lensky visited
His neighbor's unpretentious gravestone
And breathed a sigh above the dead.
He mourned him with sincerity.
"Poor Yorick!" he said mournfully,
"He used to hold me, as a child,
And many a moment I beguiled
With his Ochakov decoration.
He gave me Olga, and he'd say,
'Shall I be here to see the day?'"
And thereupon, his inspiration
Wakened by grief, Vladimir penned
An elegy upon his friend.

38

Then with another sad inscription
He paid the patriarchal dust
Of his own parents tearful tribute.
Alas! that generations must
By laws inscrutable and sealed
Like some brief harvest in the field
Rise up, mature, and die again,
Surrendering to other men!
So our ephemeral human race
Will wax and stew and seethe and boil
And finally, in great turmoil,
Themselves fill up their fathers' place.
And our own children, even so,
Will crowd us out, and we must go.

39

But meanwhile drink your fill of living,
Abortive as it is, my friends!
I know its emptiness and folly
And care but little how it ends.
I closed my eyes long since to dreams,
And yet one hope far distant seems
At times to agitate my heart:
I should be sorry to depart
And be entirely forgot.
I do not covet great renown,
Yet I am not averse, I own,
To singing of my mournful lot
So that one line of poetry,
Like a true friend, may speak of me.

40

Somewhere some heart may be affected,
And so the verses I create
May not be drowned at last in Lethe
But be preserved by fickle fate.
Perhaps—oh, flattering hope—some day
A future ignoramus may
Point to my picture and declare,
"You see a genuine poet there!"
Receive my grateful salutations,
You lover of the Grecian Nine,
Whose memory may yet enshrine
My brief and fugitive creations,
Whose reverent hands may yet caress
An old man's bays with tenderness!

Canto THREE

Elle étoit fille, elle étoit amoureuse.
—MALFILÂTRE.

1

"Where to? These poets are beyond me!"—
"Goodbye, Eugene, I have to go."—
"I won't detain you, but where do you
  Spend all your evenings, may I know?"—
"I go to see the Larins."—"What
  A curious thing! And is it not
  A task to kill the evenings there?"—
"Not in the least."—"Well, I despair
  Of understanding you! I know
  What it is like. Confess to me:
  A simple Russian family,
  Courtesies in an overflow,
  Preserves, and talk that never stops—
  The rain, the cattle, and the crops."—

2

"Still I don't see what harm is in it."—
"Being bored is harm enough, my friend."—
"I hate your modern world: far sweeter
  The fireside group, where I may spend . . ."
"An eclogue! My dear fellow, make
  An end of that, for Heaven's sake.
  Well, so you're going; that's too bad.
  But listen, Lensky, I'd be glad
  To meet this maid who seems to call
  Forth tears and verse, your Phyllida,
  Your idol, your *etcetera*.
  May I?"—"You're joking."—"Not at all."—
"Delighted!"—"When?"—"Why not tonight?
  They will receive us with delight."—

3

"Let's go." And off the two have galloped.
They reach the house, and instantly
Become recipients of a heavy
Old-fashioned hospitality.
The well-known rites at once begin:
Preserves in saucers are brought in,
And on the table they produce
A jug of huckleberry juice,
For country people eat all day.
With arms akimbo at each door
The maids stare at the bachelor,
The neighbor they must all survey;
While the strange horses in the yard
Sustain the horseboys' cool regard.

4

Then by the shortest road they hurried
Off homeward. Now let us proceed
To listen slyly to our heroes
As they dash on at topmost speed.
"Well, then, Eugene? You're yawning now!"—
"It's habit, Lensky."—"But somehow
You seem more bored than ever."—"No,
The same. How dark the meadows grow!
Make haste, make haste, Andrushka, do!
What stupid country! By the way,
Old Madame Larin, I must say,
Is simple, but she's charming, too.
That huckleberry juice, I see,
Is going to disagree with me.

5

"But tell me which of the two sisters
  I saw tonight is this Tatyana?"—
"The one who sat beside the window,
  Somber and silent, like Svyetlana."—
"It's not the younger whom you've won?"—
"Why not?"—"I'd choose the other one
  Were I a poet in your place.
  There is no life in Olga's face;
  Like a Madonna of Van Dyck,
  Expressionless and round and red
  As the dull moon above your head
  In that dull sky I so dislike."
  Vladimir made a curt reply
  And then was silent totally.

6

Meanwhile Onegin's brief appearance
  With Lensky as the Larins' guest
  Had made a great impression on them
  And roused the neighbors' interest.
  Conjecture followed on conjecture;
  They all began to tease and lecture
  And slyly, with some malice, planned
  A suitor for Tatyana's hand.
  Some even said they'd been assured
  The marriage was arranged. The date
  Would soon be fixed, but they must wait
  Till modern rings could be procured.
  Young Lensky's choice of bride-to-be
  Of course was common property.

7

Tatyana heard with some vexation
The gossip; yet it came to fill
Her heart with an inexplicable
And secret joy against her will.
A thought was born, unvoiced and dumb:
She was in love; her time had come!
So seed pods in the fires of spring
Kindle to life and blossoming.
For dreams that wasted her with burning
Desire, infusing through her blood
A craving for the fateful food,
And made her young breast throb with
    yearning—
All this had long ago begun:
Her soul was waiting for—someone.

8

So she had waited. Then she opened
Her eyes and knew that it was he!
And days and nights and lonely waking
Were now a strange perplexity
Replete with him. To our sweet maiden
All things were by some magic laden
With signs of him. Now she was bored
By the most kindly spoken word
Or by the servants' plainly shown
Concern. So in a sad unrest
She paid no heed to any guest,
But cursed the leisure they were prone
To spend in sudden calls which they
Dragged out to an unending stay.

9

With what attention she pored over
A sentimental novel! She
Drank in with what intense enjoyment
Each sweet, seductive phantasy!
For to these figures life had come
Through her dream's happy medium—
The lover of Julie Wolmar,
Malek-Adhel and de Linar,
Werther, who played the rebel's part,
And that sleep-bringing paragon,
The still unrivaled Grandison.
But to our dreamer's tender heart
Each one of them had taken on
Onegin's face and form alone.

10

Herself the heroine in fancy
Of all her favorite authors' tales,—
Delphine and Julie and Clarissa,—
Tatyana walks the woods and vales,
Alone but for her dangerous book;
And searching there she seems to look
On her own dream in counterpart,
Fruits of an overflowing heart.
She understands their sorrows better
For hers, and they become her own.
She sighs and in an undertone
Repeats her favorite hero's letter;
But Grandison, just let me say,
Was not our hero, anyway.

11

Tuning his style to solemn measures,
The ardent author used to plan
To make his hero an example
Of all perfection in one man.
This youth, the wrongfully oppressed,
His loving maker would invest
With all fine feeling, wit, and grace,
And with a very handsome face.
The enraptured hero was resigned
To making every sacrifice
To passion, at whatever price,
And in conclusion you would find
The wicked dealt his just reward,
The good man's happiness restored.

12

But nowadays our minds are cloudy
And morals bore us through and through;
In novels, even, vice is pleasant
And there it is triumphant, too.
The British Muse's fancies creep
Into the adolescent's sleep
And maids revere as idols now
Some Vampire with a pensive brow,
Melmoth, the gloomy vagabond,
The Corsair, or the Wandering Jew,
Sbogar and all his retinue.
Lord Byron with his happy wand
Has clothed in dark romanticism
Incorrigible egotism.

13
But what, my friends, does all this lead to?
It may be, Heaven will decree
That I shall cease to be a poet,
For a new devil dwells in me
And, scorning Phoebus' threats,—who
    knows?—
I may descend to simple prose:
A novel of old-fashioned ways
Will fill my cheerful latter days.
I shall not try to make you see
The secret agonies of sin,
But I shall represent therein
Scenes from some Russian family,
Innocent dreams of love enraptured,
The olden days and deeds recaptured.

14
I'll write about a simple father
Or some old uncle, in my book;
The children's secret assignations
Beneath the lindens, by the brook;
Torments of wretched jealousy,
Partings and tears,—then harmony.
One final quarrel I'll allow,
Then they shall take the marriage vow.
I shall recall once more the sweet
And tortured language of desire,
The words that love and pain inspire
Once spoken at my mistress' feet
In former days when I was young,
But now grown strange upon my tongue.

15

But oh, Tatyana, dear Tatyana!
The tears are gathering in my eyes;
Already to a modern despot
You've given yourself as sacrifice.
You will be lost, my dear, but first
You'll call up in a dazzling burst
Of hope this unknown happiness
And taste the joy life may possess.
You drink love's poison, strange and heating,
And all becomes a phantasy—
You look, and everywhere you see
A trysting place for happy meeting,
And every hour in every place
You see the fatal tempter's face.

16

Her love and longing plague Tatyana.
She walks the garden paths and grieves,
Then shuts her staring eyes, too weary
To take a step. Her bosom heaves,
A flush spreads quickly on her cheek,
Her breath stops short, she cannot speak,
A flashing blinds her, and she hears
A sudden roaring in her ears...
The night has fallen; on its round
The far moon traverses the sky,
The nightingale from woods near by
Sends out a flood of piercing sound.
But sleep though longed for is perverse:
Tatyana whispers to her nurse.

17

"Oh, nurse, I cannot sleep; it's airless!
  Open the window and sit near!"—
"What is it, Tanya, what's the matter?"—
"Let's talk of olden days, nurse dear!"—
"What shall I say? I used to know
  A lot of tales of long ago,
  Of demons who would cast a blight
  On maidens out of wicked spite,
  But Tanya, that's all dim to me
  And I've forgotten what I knew;
  Bad times have come; it's all too true
  That I have lost my memory..."
"But tell me, nurse, in days long gone
  Were you in love with anyone?"—

18

"Oh, Tanya, stop it! Why, of loving
  I never heard a single breath!
  And if I had, my husband's mother
  Would have tormented me to death."—
"But nurse, how did you marry, then?"—
"As the Lord wills it among men:
  I was just thirteen years, all told,
  My Vanya was not quite so old;
  About two weeks the matchmaker
  Came to my father's house, and he
  Gave me his blessing finally
  And I wept bitterly for fear.
  They loosed my braids with lamentation
  And then to church with jubilation.

19

"I went to my new home, a stranger—
  But you don't hear a word I say."—
"Oh, nurse, oh, nurse, I am so wretched!
  I'm all upset, my dear, today.
  At any minute I could weep."—
"You're sick, my child. May Heaven keep
  And comfort you! There, Tanya, tell
  Me what to get to make you well!
  You're feverish, all your talk is wild,
  I'll bring some holy water."—"Oh,
  I am not ill—but nurse, you know—
  I am in love."—"God help you, child."
  And, her hand trembling in the air,
  She made a cross and said a prayer.

20

"I am in love," Tatyana whispered
  Once more, and made a little moan.
"You are not well, my own, my darling."—
"I am in love; leave me alone."
  And all the while the still moon shone,
  Illumining with its soft tone
  Tatyana's pallid beauty where
  She lay in tears with loosened hair;
  While on the bench beside her bed
  The old nurse sat, so small and white,
  Wrapped in a long robe for the night,
  A kerchief tied about her head,
  And the whole house lay in a swoon
  Beneath the enchantment of the moon.

21

Tatyana gazing at the moonlight
Was borne far off in dreams. And soon
A sudden thought arose within her...
"Nurse, go away, leave me alone.
A pen and paper but no light,
And put the table near. Good night!"
She is alone in the still room
Which the moon makes half light, half
    gloom;
Propped on her elbow she writes on;
Eugene alone fills all her heart
And from her words devoid of art
Pure love breathes forth. Now it is done.
She folds it. Oh, Tatyana, who
Will read this letter sent by you?

22

I have known supercilious beauties
As cold and pure as winter snow,
Merciless, matchless, without blemish,
Impossible for man to know;
I've marveled at such worth inborn
And at their fashionable scorn
And then I've run away in dread;
For on their foreheads I had read,
Bright as some hellish diadem,
"Abandon hope forever." They
Inspire love with great dismay;
To terrify is joy for them.
Perhaps upon the Neva's shore
You've met such ladies long before.

23

And I have been the faithful follower
Of ladies of capricious ways
Completely, selfishly indifferent
To lovers' sighs and lovers' praise.
And I have seen to my surprise
When their stern bearing and cold eyes
Had forced shy love away, they then
Knew how to waken it again.
At least some touch of sympathy,
A tenderer cadence in the voice,
Would cause their suitors to rejoice,
And with a blind credulity
The young adorer would once more
Pursue his charming conqueror.

24

Why should Tatyana seem more faulty?
Because in her simplicity,
Believing in her chosen idol,
She had no thought of trickery?
Because she did not play a part,
But loved and yielded to her heart?
Because the fates had given her
A most confiding character,
A fancy full of warmth and yearning,
A stubborn head and mother wit,
A will robust and definite,
A heart that was both soft and burning?
You must forgive her indiscretion
And the rash form of its expression.

25

Coquettes take all these matters coolly:
Tatyana loved so much that she
Was like a charming child renouncing
Herself to love entirely.
She did not say: "I'll make him wait
So he may set a higher rate
On love and fall into my net.
I'll flatter him at first to whet
His pride with hope and then profess
Perplexity and wring his heart
So that his jealous fears may start;
For sometimes, bored with much success,
The cunning prisoner will tear
His bonds apart and break the snare."

26

I have another task to finish
Or bring my native land to shame:
I must translate Tatyana's letter
Because her Russian was so lame.
She did not read our magazines
And did not move by any means
With ease or gracefulness among
The mazes of her mother tongue.
And so she wrote in French. Alas!
No Russian lady hitherto
In love, I must repeat to you,
Would think her country's speech would pass
When she desired to compose
A fine epistolary prose.

27

I know some people want the ladies
To read in Russian. It's a risk!
Picture them skimming *Good Intentions*
With interest both cool and brisk!
Dear poets, I refer to you!
For, tell me, the sweet creatures who
Were, for your sins, your universe,
The secret subjects of your verse,
The goddesses who ruled your heart—
Confess, was not their Russian so
Laborious and weak and slow
And mispronounced with so much art
That on their lips the foreign speech
Seemed like the native tongue of each?

28

God send I never meet a lady
Academician at a ball,
Or on the steps take tender leave of
A seminarist in a shawl.
I do not like red lips that pout
Nor Russian words pronounced without
A grammar slip. And yet some day
The newer race of beauties may,
To my misfortune, introduce
A taste for grammar's niceties,
Hearing the journals' cogent pleas,
And usher verses into use.
But as for me, my lot is cast—
I shall be faithful to the past.

29

Inaccurate and careless prattle
With all the words accented wrong
Will always cause my heart to tremble
Within me, as it has so long.
No strength is left me to retreat,
And Gallicisms are as sweet
To me as youth long past, perverse
As Bogdanovich and his verse.
But let's go on— I must attack
The letter of my heroine:
I gave my word, but I begin
To wish that I might take it back,
For Parny and the gentle phrase
Are out of fashion nowadays.

30

Singer of banquets and of sadness,
If you were here, I would have pressed
Our former friendship into service
And made an indiscreet request:
To take this young girl's passionate
But foreign words and to translate
Them to some magic melody.
Where are you? Come! For I agree
To cede you with my compliments
My rights.— But heedless of the praise
He used to love in other days,
Alone and silent, he frequents
The barren cliffs of Finland's shore
And heeds my mournful cry no more.

31

Tatyana's letter is before me:
I guard it like a sacred thing,
And as I read its pages over
I feel a secret suffering.
Who was it taught her to express
This jumble of sweet foolishness?
How did she learn this tender art,
The nonsense of a loving heart,
So charming and so perilous?
I do not know, but here I place
My poor translation like a face
Sketched by a weak and timorous
Designer: "Freischütz" rendered by
Beginner's fingers, stiff and shy.

* * *

TATYANA'S LETTER TO ONEGIN

I write you. If I took an hour
I could not make myself more plain,
And now you have it in your power
To punish me with your disdain.
But if you find you have for me
The smallest drop of sympathy
You will not leave me in such pain.
At first I wanted to keep still;
Indeed, you never would have heard
Of my disgrace a single word
If I had thought, "Perhaps he will
Call on us, if but once a week,
And once more I shall hear him speak,

*However rarely." If I might
Answer you just a word and then
Go dreaming of your face again
Till our next meeting, day and night!
They say you are a misanthrope
And find our village life a bore.—
To dazzle you we could not hope,
But you were welcome at our door.*

*Why did you ever come to call?
For in this far, forgotten spot
We never should have met at all
And all this pain, so burning hot,
I might have missed ... And then, why not?
As I grew calm, as people do,
I might have found in later life
A mate and been a faithful wife
And a devoted mother, too.*

*But no! There is no other man
To whom I could have given my love,
And I am yours by Heaven's plan
Determined in the courts above.
My life so far has been a pledge
Of this sure meeting God would send;
To love you is my privilege,
You are my guardian to the end.
You came to me in dreams at first
And, dimly seen, you still were dear,
Your voice was lovely to my ear,
Your eyes awoke a longing thirst.*

That was no dream so long ago!
You came—and instantly I knew!
I was confused but all aglow;
My heart said, "It is he, I know."
Did I not use to talk with you?
You spoke to me when all was still,
When I was out among the poor,
Or when I used to say a prayer
To ease my mind, so sore and ill.
And at those moments, dearest dream,
Was it not you who came to gleam
From out the dark translucency
And bending down so softly, shed
Your love and joy around my bed,
Whispering words of hope to me?
Are you my guardian angel or
A sly, seductive counselor?
Oh, settle all these doubts for me!
It may be vanity and lies
Have cheated my simplicity
And it is destined otherwise ...
But be that as it may! For all
My life I give you my affection.
I feel my tears begin to fall
As I beseech you for protection.
For think! I am as if alone;
No one here guesses what I feel;
My senses have begun to reel
And all my love must die unknown.
I write you now: one glance from you
Can kindle hope within my heart
Or tear these dreadful dreams apart
With your reproach, deserved, I know.

I've done. I dare not read it through;
I am half dead with fear and shame,
But I will trust myself to you
With confidence, in honor's name.

* * *

32

The paper trembles as she holds it . . .
Tatyana gives a little sigh;
Upon her feverish tongue the tablet
To seal her letter still is dry.
Her charming head begins to sway,
Her light nightgown has slipped away
And left one shoulder all unveiled.
But now the brilliant moon has paled,
The valley lightens toward the morn,
The stream becomes a distant blur
Of silver, and the villager
Is wakened by the shepherd's horn.
The world is up and night is done;
But to Tatyana all is one.

33

She does not see the morning brighten
Nor seal her letter, but instead,
Oblivious of all around her,
Sits idly on with drooping head.
Then softly opening the door,
Gray-haired Philipyevna once more
Comes in with tea upon a tray:
"Get up, my child, another day!

But you've already waked, my dear!
My little early bird! Last night
You gave me such an awful fright,
But now, thank God, I needn't fear.
It hasn't left a single trace
Upon your poppy-blossom face!"

34

"Do something for me, nurse, I beg you."—
"Of course, my child. What is it, though?"—
"Don't hesitate—don't think about it,
  You see...Oh, nurse, please don't say no!"—
"God knows I'll do it for your sake."—
"Then have your grandson go and take
  This note, but do it quietly...
  To O...our neighbor...Tell him he
  Must be most careful not to say
  A word of me."—"My darling, who
  Is it that he's to take it to?
  Dear heart, my wits have gone astray...
  We have so many neighbors here
  I can't keep track of them, my dear."—

35

"Oh, nurse, you are so foolish."—"Darling,
  I've grown so old, so very old...
  Our wits get dull with living, Tanya.
  I used to do as I was told
  Quick as they got the order out."—
"Oh, nurse, what is this all about?
  What do I care about your wits?

This is about Onegin—it's
A letter to him."—"All right, then,
But don't be angry sweet; we grow
So dull as we get old, you know.
But why are you so pale again?"—
"It's nothing, nurse, I'm well today...
But send your grandson right away."

36

But all day long there was no answer.
Another day of martyrdom;
Pale as a shadow, dressed since morning,
Tatyana waits: "When will it come?"
Now Olga's suitor has arrived.
"Where is your friend? He has deprived
Us of his wit this many a day,"
Tatyana hears her mother say.
She trembled and turned very red.
"He said he'd be here without fail.
I don't know... possibly the mail
Detained him somewhat," Lensky said.
Tatyana, listening, dropped her eyes
As if rebuked by these replies.

37

Twilight, and shining on the table
The evening samovar aboil,
Warming the china teapot on it
In clouds of steam that twist and coil.
Already Olga busily
Sets out the cups, and now the tea

Descends, a dark and fragrant stream,
While a boy passes round the cream.
Beside the window, breathing on
The chilly panes, Tatyana stood
Bemused, poor child, and where she could
With her small finger she had drawn
Upon the misted glass a row
Of sacred letters, *E* and *O*.

38

But all the time her heart was aching,
Her eyes half blind. An unforeseen
Clatter— Her blood stood still— Now
    nearer—
They've halted in the yard. Eugene!
"Oh!" And more lightly than a shade
Through hall and porch and yard she made
Her flight to where the gardens wound . . .
On, on, and dared not once turn round.
Past bush and grove and bridge she flashed,
The pathway to the lake, the lawn;
Tearing the lilacs, she has gone
On over flower beds and dashed
Down to the little rivulet
Where, breathless, on a bench she let

39

Herself drop down. "He's here! Oh, Heavens!
Eugene . . . What does he think of me?"
And now her heart, though aching, shelters
A dim dream of felicity.

She trembles, and her pulses pound.
Oh, is that he? No, not a sound!
She sees the servant girls whose heads
Are bent above the currant beds,
Singing in chorus while they pick
The berries, singing which they do
Because they have been ordered to.
Such is the cunning squire's trick:
Sly mouths engaged in this pursuit
Will not eat up the master's fruit.

* * *

SERVANT GIRLS' SONG

Lovely maidens, maidens gay,
Darlings, sweethearts, come and play!
Let us play together, maidens,
Darlings, let us dance and play.
Let us sing a little song,
Sing a magic little song,
Lead some boy on with a glance
Till he joins our circle-dance.
When we've called him from afar,
When he's followed where we are,
Let us scatter, maidens sweet!
Then we'll stone the boy with cherries,
Cherries and with red raspberries,
Currants red and good to eat.
Do not come so near and try
To hear the secret words we say,
Do not come so near to spy
On the games that maidens play.

40

Tatyana scarcely hears their voices
Which her own tumult seems to drown,
But waits with an extreme impatience
Until her heart shall quiet down
And her cheeks lose their bright carnation.
But still she shakes in agitation
And brighter still the scarlet streaks
Flame out upon her brilliant cheeks.
Just so a butterfly, forlorn
And glittering in a schoolboy's net,
Will beat its rainbow wings and fret;
So a small hare in winter corn
Will shake when suddenly it sees
A hunter hiding in the trees.

41

But finally and breathing deeply
She got up from the bench to go,
And as she started down the pathway,
Before her face, his eyes aglow,
She saw Eugene ... For there he stood,
Like some grim shadow from the wood;
And she, as if bereft of will
Or scorched by fire, stood quite still.
But now I think I shall defer
Until I feel I have more strength
The telling you at greater length
Just what the consequences were.
Some other day I'll do my best,
But now I'll walk a while and rest.

Canto FOUR

*La morale est dans la nature
des choses.*

—NECKER.

1

IN YOUNGER DAYS the artful, charming,
And weaker sex ruled over me
And I obeyed their slightest wishes
Like some immutable decree.
My heart and mind were all aflame,
And to my vision woman came
Like some pure goddess who possessed
My soul—perfection manifest,
Where nothing could be found amiss.
I never thought that I could capture
Her love, but in a silent rapture
Beheld in her ideal bliss.
To live and die at her dear feet—
I could not ask a fate more sweet.

2

Then suddenly I came to hate her
And wept and trembled; now I saw
In her with horror the creation
Of some mysterious, evil law.
Her piercing glance of invitation,
Her smile, her voice, her conversation,
Were treacherous and wicked things.
She had drunk deep at poisoned springs
And hungered for my martyrdom
And tears, subsisting on my blood.
Then suddenly again she stood
A marble figure, cold and dumb,
Before Pygmalion as he prayed
That she might be a living maid.

3

I too, like the prophetic poet,
Might sing the names he loved to write—
Of Lilith, Daphne, and Temira—
They're dreams long vanished from my
    sight.
There was but one among them all
Who ever kept me at her call.
Was I in love? With whom? And where,
And for how long? ... Why should you care?
That's not the point. But what has been
Has been, and is not any more.
But since those days I've closed the door
To love, and all is dark within
My heart, which, long untenanted,
Is desolate and cold and dead.

4

I've found the ladies cannot marvel
Sufficiently at us—(Here I
Betray a spiritual secret)—
They do not rate themselves so high!
The raptures to which they give birth
Appear to them a cause for mirth;
And we must own our amorous
Behavior is ridiculous.
We are their slaves in word and act
And madly think they will accord
Their love in virtuous reward,
As if we somehow could exact
Deep feelings and impassioned sighs
From lilies or from butterflies.

5, 6, 7

The less we care about a woman
The easier to touch her heart
And bring about her final ruin
With our strategic, cheating art.
Cold-blooded rakishness was hailed
Of old as love, and never failed
To boast its triumphs beyond measure
And, without love, to take its pleasure.
But such enjoyments seem at last
More worthy old baboons, and we
Consign them to their century:
The day of libertines has passed
Along with red heels and the big
Majestic powdered periwig.

8

Who will not tire of deceiving,
Of saying one thing a hundred ways?
Of proving what has long been granted
By all, with many a solemn phrase?
Of conquering a prejudice
That no young thirteen-year-old miss
Has ever felt or ever will,
And hear the ancient scruples still?
And who will not be bored with lies,
Pretended terror, vows, and prayers,
Notes six sheets long and threats and tears,
Rings, gossip, and the watchful eyes
Of aunts and mothers and, still worse,
The friendship that the husbands nurse?

9

All this was my Eugene's opinion;
For he had been in days of old
The victim of impetuous fancies
And passions wild and uncontrolled.
Spoiled by a world replete with guile,
He sought one thing a little while,
Then fled from it in bitterness,
Worn out by longing and success—
Success too lightly won by half.
And yet alone or in a crowd
He heard his heart complain aloud,
And hid his yawns beneath a laugh.
So eight years, wild and turbulent,
Slipped by, and his best youth was spent.

10

He did not fall in love with beauties
These days, but still kept in the race.
Refused, he soon found consolation;
Deceived, he took a breathing space.
He sought them out in lukewarm fashion,
Forsaking them without compassion,
Regardless of their love or hate,
Like some chance caller coming late
For evening whist, just interested
Enough to sit and play a game,
Then leave as calmly as he came
To go at once to home and bed,
Who, when the day breaks, hardly knows
Where it will find him at its close.

11

But Tanya's letter moved Onegin
To an unwonted sympathy;
The language of her maiden daydream
Gave rise to tranquil revery,
And he recalled Tatyana's fair
Pale face and melancholy air,
And plunged into a pleasant stream
Of innocent and gentle dream.
Perhaps his old-time hot emotion
Possessed him for a little while,
And yet he would not work with guile
Upon a simple girl's devotion.
So now we're at the garden scene
In which Tatyana met Eugene.

12

The first few moments, they were silent;
But then Onegin, drawing near,
Began: "You wrote me, don't deny it,
And I hold all you uttered dear,
As the confiding, innocent
Expression of a sentiment
Which comes, I know it, from your heart,
So that emotions seemed to start
Within me that were long unknown.
I do not mean to flatter you
But to reply in words as true
And unaffected as your own.
Take my confession. You are free
To think just as you will of me.

13

"If life within the narrow circle
  Of family cares had been my goal:
  If pleasant fate had ordered for me
  A husband's or a father's rôle:
  If for one moment I had been
  Enamored of the fireside scene,
  I never could have hoped to find
  A wife more suited to my mind.
  And had I found you, I confess
  Quite plainly it is you alone
  I would have chosen for my own,
  The promise of all loveliness,
  And I should be, with you for prize,
  As happy as within me lies.

14

"But I was never fortune's darling
  And I am strange to happiness;
  I am unworthy your perfections
  And me your love can never bless.
  Oh, on my conscience, credit me,
  For us a married life would be
  A torment, and however much
  I loved you, it would end, for such
  Is habit's force. You'd weep; but far
  From moving me your tears would but
  Seal up a heart already shut.
  Then judge just what the roses are
  That Hymen would be apt to strew
  Throughout the years for me and you.

15

"For what in life can be more wretched
 Than some poor wife who makes her moan
 In sorrow for her worthless husband
 And spends her days and nights alone?
 While her dull husband, though he knows
 Her merits, coldly jealous, goes
 About in inarticulate
 Displeasure, and reviles his fate.
 Just such a sullen wretch am I.
 And when you wrote me with the whole
 Pure ardor of your simple soul,
 Would this have seemed to satisfy
 Your dreams? Can this indeed be what
 Stern fate has destined for your lot?

16

"The years do not return, nor visions,
 And so my heart can never be
 Renewed. I love you like a brother,
 Or, as I think, more tenderly.
 But don't be angry when I say
 That a young girl quite often may
 Indulge a passing dream and then
 Change it for someone else again,
 Just as a sapling takes new leaf;
 And you will fall in love once more,
 So Heaven wills; but heed me, for
 Such inexperience leads to grief:
 Not everyone will understand,
 And you must learn more self-command."

17

Thus did Eugene pronounce his sermon,
While scarcely breathing, blinded by
Her tears, Tatyana, without protest
Attended to his homily.
Then silently she took her way
(Mechanically, as they say),
Weighing upon the arm he lent,
Her small head sorrowfully bent,
Back through the kitchen-garden, home.
And no one thought on seeing this
Companionship it was amiss,
So free were all to go and come:
The country has its pleasant rule
No less than Moscow's haughty school.

18

You must agree with me, dear reader,
Our friend has acted kindly by
Tatyana, and has manifested
A genuine nobility
Of feeling, although people may
With much ill will be heard to say
The most remorseless calumnies,
His friends, as well as enemies
(And possibly they are the same),
Abusing him. We all must have
Our enemies, of course, but save
Us from our friends, in Heaven's name!
These friends of ours! They well may be
Preserved by us in memory!

19

But why? It's nothing! For such empty
And dismal thoughts I have no space.
And I shall only say in passing
There is no lie, however base,
Born in a den of calumny
And fostered by society:
There is no sort of foolish sham
Nor any vulgar epigram
That with a smile your friend will not
Repeat, in well-bred circles, too,
With his mistakes tacked on, of you.
And yet he has no slanderous plot—
He'd be your shield through thick and thin,
He loves you so, like your own kin.

20

Hm! hm! And now, distinguished reader,
How are your family? All well?
And here perhaps you will permit me
To take a little time to tell
Just what I mean by family.
Our relatives are those whom we
Are bound in duty to caress,
To honor and sincerely bless
And call upon on Christmas Day
As custom bids; or if we fail
In that, to wish them well by mail,
So that on other days they may
Forget us with their conscience clear.
God grant they live for many a year!

21

But gentle beauties hold us longer
Than friendship or than family ties;
And even in the stormiest weather
Their power you will recognize.
Of course ... But fashion, never still—
A natural leaning toward self-will—
What people say about the town—
And the fair sex is light as down!
And any virtuous wife, beside,
Subjects herself to the dominion
And heeds her husband's least opinion;
And so the friend whom you relied
Upon so long is snatched away:
To joke with love is Satan's way.

22

Then whom are we to love and trust in
And count on never to abuse
Our love, but measure all our actions
With the same yardstick that we use?
Who will not slander us, but take
The greatest pains for our dear sake?
Who never bores us, but exalts
Us always, even for our faults?
You restless seeker of a dream,
It is yourself you must adore!
Don't waste your labor any more,
Reader, for you yourself would seem
The object to be placed above
All else, and worthiest your love.

23

What followed on Tatyana's meeting
With our Eugene? We all can guess!
The foolish pangs of love continued
To stir and trouble her no less,
And poor Tatyana feels the smart
Of greedy grief within her heart
More burning and more desperate,
While sleep forsakes her, soon and late.
Her smile, her maiden calm, the spring
Of health and joy in all around
Have vanished like an empty sound
And Tanya's youth is withering.
So shadows of a storm cloud may
Beset the bright and newborn day.

24

Alas, Tatyana droops in silence,
She fades and withers visibly;
Nothing now interests her, nothing
Can rouse her from despondency.
Shaking their heads, the neighbors say
In solemn conclave every day,
"High time she married, time indeed!"
But now, enough. I'll make what speed
I can to paint a gayer kind
Of cheerful love; and yet I still
Am saddened quite against my will
For Tanya, who still fills my mind.
Forgive me, I have always been
In love with my dear heroine.

25

From hour to hour yet more enchanted
With Olga, young and fair to see,
Vladimir gave his heart up wholly
To her in sweet captivity.
Forever with her, in the gloom
Of twilight sitting in her room,
Or in the garden arm in arm
Walking in all the morning's charm—
And then what else? Perplexed and seized
With shame and hopelessly ensnared,
The most that he had ever dared
(And that when Olga smiled and teased)
Was just to smooth a loosened curl
Or kiss the dress of his dear girl.

26

Sometimes he read aloud to Olga
A moralistic tale by one
Who knew of nature more than even
Chateaubriand himself had known.
And now and then when he would find
Fancies unsuited to a mind
So virginal, all wind and rage,
He blushingly would skip a page.
And there were many hours when
Leaning above a game of chess
They'd sit absorbed and motionless,
Away from everyone again,
And Lensky with an absent look
Would check his own king with his rook.

27

And when at home, it still is Olga
Who occupies his fancy there;
He fills the odd leaves of her album
With sketches drawn with loving care:
A country scene, perhaps a tomb,
A Cyprian temple steeped in gloom
And next a dove upon a lute
In ink, and colored up to suit;
And on the written sheets below
The signatures of others, he
Would write a verse in, tenderly,
A silent monument to show
Long afterward when years had gone
How momentary thoughts live on.

28

You've doubtless often seen the album
Of some provincial miss and found
It filled with all her girl friends' scribbles,
Above, across, and all around,
Heedless of spelling; countless rhymes
Come down to us from older times
And here set forth as friendship's token,
Curtailed or lengthened out or broken.
So on the first page you will find:
"Qu'écrirez-vous sur ces tablettes?"
Beneath it, *"t. à. v. Annette"*;
And on the last page, duly signed:
"Who loves you more devotedly
  Will sign your album after me."

29

Here you will certainly discover
A torch and flowers and two hearts,
And you will probably decipher
The vows "of love till death us parts";
While here and there some army wit
Has scrawled his caustic verse in it.
In such an album, friends, I write,
I will admit it, with delight,
Because I feel so sure meanwhile
That all my well-meant foolery
Will be regarded leniently
And that they will not later smile
Ironically and decide
How cleverly they think I lied.

30

But you, odd volumes from the devil's
Own library, resplendent books
Which are the torment of the rhymesters
Of fashion, you whose handsome looks
Baratynsky has brought about,
Or Tolstoy's brush, I could cry out
For thunderbolts of God to smite
And burn you all to ash some night.
For when some sumptuous *grande dame*
Hands me her quarto with the page
Ready to write on, quivering rage
Lays hold of me; an epigram
Stirs in me, sharp and critical,
While they expect a madrigal.

31

They are not madrigals that Lensky
Indites for Olga's benefit;
His verses breathe out love and sweetness
And not a cold and sparkling wit.
Whatever he may hear or see
Of Olga fills his poetry;
Reflecting simple truth, his song
Flows ever placidly along.
Just so in heartfelt ecstasies,
Inspired Yazykov, do you too
Extol some goddess, God knows who,
And all your precious elegies
Will some day tell again the whole
Life story of your poet's soul.

32

But listen! Hear the critic sternly
Demand we throw away for good
The humble elegiac garland!
And to our rhyming brotherhood
He cries:"Now stop this whimpering
And croaking of the same old thing,
This mourning always for the past.
Enough! Sing something else at last."
You're right; and you'll point out instead
The pipe, the dagger, and the mask,
And from old stores of thought you'll ask
That we should resurrect the dead.
Is that not it? "No, take your pen
And write us odes now, gentlemen!

33

"Such as in old and hardy ages
 The poets used to undertake..."
 What, only odes the proud and solemn!
 Come, friend, what difference does it make?
 Think what the satirist has said!
 Can you prefer to read instead
 Of our own rhymesters' somber mode
 The strained and foreign-tempered ode?
"But elegies are vain and light,
 They have so pitiful an aim,
 While odes are noble and can claim
 A lofty purpose..." Here I might
 Take issue, were my inclinations
 To quarrel with two generations.

34

A votary of fame and freedom,
In the wild turmoil fancy brings
Vladimir would have taken gladly
To odes, had Olga read such things.
Has ever poet had the chance
To read his fables of romance
Before his love? The world can hold
No greater bounty, we are told.
How blest the timid lover seeing
Himself read out his dreams before
The object whom his songs adore,
A sweetly silent, lovely being!
Though thoughts quite other may engage
Her mind than those upon his page.

35

But all the harvest of my dreaming
And my essays in harmony
My old nurse heard alone, my childhood's
Most faithful friend; or possibly
If some chance neighbor happened in
To a dull dinner, I'd begin,
Catching him by his coat lapel,
And let my tragic numbers swell
To his dismay. But jokes aside,
When verse and longing overtake
My heart, I walk beside the lake
Until the wild ducks, terrified,
Hearing my sounding strophes ring,
Fly far away on flapping wing.

36

They're almost out of sight. A hunter
Within the wood, his care undone,
Damns poetry and whistles softly,
Taking his finger from his gun.
To every man his favorite game,
His best-loved pastime: one will aim
At ducks to test his musketry,
Another rave in verse, like me,
While one man bats impertinent flies,
Another to great wars is vowed,
And one with wisdom rules the crowd,
And pampered feeling occupies
Another man, or wine; and still
The good is mingled with the ill.

37

But what about Eugene? My brothers,
Be patient with my loitering way!
I will describe in every item
The occupations of his day.
Onegin was an anchorite:
In summer at seven when day was bright
He walked out lightly dressed to where
The stream flowed by the hill and there,
As once Gulnare's creator, swam
This Hellespont of his, and then,
Back with his coffee-cup again,
He'd skim a page, some poor flimflam,
And dress. But please take this from me:
You never wore such clothes as he!

38

A Russian smock, and for a girdle
A handkerchief of silk to wrap
Around; a Tatar coat unbuttoned,
And lastly a white-vizored cap,
And that was all. By this strange dress,
Immoral and insane, no less,
A Madame Durin not far off
As well as one Mizinchikov,
A squire who lived near by, were both
Incensed. Eugene was either blind
Or simply too remiss to mind
Their talk, and he would have been loath
To change, for that involved such labor:
A most insufferable neighbor!

39

Long walks, and books, and sleep unbroken,
The shady woods, the murmuring brooks,
A kiss at times from some fair maiden,
Dark-eyed, with bright and youthful looks;
A swift-paced horse that knew his hand;
A dinner rather nicely planned;
A bottle of a good light wine
And solitude and peace divine—
Such was the blameless life he led;
And imperceptibly he fell
Beneath its easy carefree spell
And quite forgot, while summer sped,
His friends, the city, and the noise
And boredom of those empty joys.

40

Our northern summer does no more than
Burlesque the winter of the south,—
One flash and over,—yet you seldom
Will hear such words escape our mouth.
The sky already breathed of fall,
The sun was rarely seen at all,
The days grew short, in mystery
The woodland shed its canopy
And stood lamenting, brown and bare.
Upon the fields a mist was spread,
The wild geese squawking overhead
Flew south in caravans, for there
Approached that month most desolate,
November, knocking at the gate.

41

The morning rises cold and misty;
No sounds of work reverberate
From off the fields; beside the roadway
A wolf runs with his hungry mate,
And, scenting him, the traveler's horse
Neighs, and his rider turns his course
On up the hill at topmost speed.
No longer does the shepherd need
To drive the cattle from the shed
At dawn, nor with his horn at noon
To call them all together. Soon
The cottage maid will spin her thread
And sing beside the crackling lights
Of pine-flares, friends of winter nights.

42

The fields were glittering with silver,
And everywhere the water froze
And cracked (Yes, here's what you're expecting,
The old romantic rhyme-word—rose!);
More neat than any parquet floor
The river gleamed, for now it wore
A dress of ice, and little boys
Went skating there with mirth and noise;
A gander with its red web-feet
Steps out upon the icy brim
Meaning to take a little swim,
And slips and falls; and gay and sweet
Like stars that flash and spin around
The first snow falls upon the ground.

43

And now what are your country pleasures?
To walk? From where the village lies,
Monotonous and drab and barren,
Against your will you turn your eyes.
To gallop over fields forlorn
And waste? Your horse in shoes too worn
May slip and fall when all around
There's only treacherous, icy ground.
To stay at home and dismally
Read your de Pradt or Walter Scott?
To do accounts and like as not
To lose your temper, drink, and see
Each night drag onward like the last?
So may your winter well be passed.

44

Onegin, like a true Childe Harold,
Is plunged in gloomy revery;
He takes an icy bath on waking,
Then gives his listless energy
Indoors, alone, to his accounts;
Or with a billiard cue surmounts
Some subtle problem with two balls
From morning until evening falls.
But then he puts his cue away
And waits, with something of desire,
The table set before the fire,
For Lensky, driven in his sleigh
With three roan horses, to come in.
Now dinner's served— and we'll begin!

45

And now the wine of blessèd Widow
Clicquot is brought, or else Moët,
In its chilled bottle, to the poet.
With all its froth and bubbling play
It's like the sparkling Hippocrene,
A symbol of so much we've seen.
It had a charm that could transcend
All else for me and I would spend
Upon it all I had on earth.
Do you recall what lunatics
We were and to what harebrained tricks
That magic liquid once gave birth?
What endless jokes and verse in streams
And wild discussions and sweet dreams!

46

But with its foam and effervescence
It's bad for my digestion, so
I now prefer to it the sober
And more judicious old Bordeaux.
I am not equal to Champagne;
It's like a mistress, light of brain,
Flighty, compounded of self-will,
Though brilliant and vivacious still.
But you, Bordeaux, are like a friend,
A comrade who is everywhere
In readiness and glad to share
Our griefs and sorrows or to spend
With us our quiet leisure days.
Bordeaux, I sing your well-earned praise!

47

The fire is going out. The ashes
Have almost veiled the glowing coal
And you can barely see the streamer
Of smoke wind upward while the whole
Black fireplace breathes gentle heat.
Two wreaths of pipe smoke rise and meet
Within the chimney. In the room
The dusk has gathered; through the gloom
The goblets sparkle merrily.
I love to feel the friendly power
Of wine and friendship at this hour
We Russians call, I can't say why,
The hour between the wolf and dog.
Now hear our two friends' dialogue.

48

"How are our neighbors? How's Tatyana?
  Your jolly Olga, how is she?"—
"Pour me another half a glassful.
  There, that's enough. The family
Are well. They sent their greetings. Oh,
How lovely Olga seems to grow!
Her neck and bosom, and then too
How sweet her soul! Come, sometime you
Must go and pay a call. And then
You know yourself it's hardly nice;
You called on them exactly twice
And never showed yourself again.
But what a fool! I said I'd speak
To you. They want you for next week."

49

"What, me?"—"Yes, Saturday they're having
Tatyana's name-day celebration;
Olenka and her mother asked you,
You can't refuse their invitation."—
"But there'll be droves of people there,
The sort of rabble I can't bear."—
"No, hardly anyone at all."—
"Who?"—"Just the relatives will call.
For my sake come. Don't be above
These parties!"—"Very well."—"That's fine!"
And drinking off a glass of wine
In honor of his ladylove
He turned, as lovers will, once more,
To Olga, his fair conqueror.

50

For he was happy. In a fortnight
The day would come, long heralded;
The crown and sweets of love and marriage,
The mystery of the bridal bed
And all its rapture would be his.
For of the boredom wedlock is,
The cares and sorrows Hymen brings—
He had no inkling of such things.
Though we, as Hymen's foes, complain
Of family life as one long scene
Of tedious doings, poor and mean,
Like a romance of La Fontaine,
Poor Lensky, with his loving heart,
Was born for a domestic part.

51

For he was loved—or so he fancied—
And he was happy in his dream.
The man who lets cold reason slumber
And rests upon his faith will seem
A hundred times more happy than
Another, like a wine-dazed man
At some poor inn; or, better still,
Like butterflies that drink their fill,
Glued to the flowers in spring. But he
Who never revels is the one
To pity, who has never done
A foolish thing, whom fantasy
Annoys, and who will not unbend,
But lives cold-hearted to the end.

Canto FIVE

*Oh, do not dream such dreadful
dreams, Sweet child, Svyetlana!*

—ZHUKOVSKY.

1

That year the autumn weather lasted
Well on through Christmastime while all
Of nature waited for the winter
And still the first snow did not fall
Till January third. That night
It came: Tatyana, waking bright
And early, looked outdoors and found
Roofs, fences, flower beds and ground
All hidden. There the magpies, gay
And cheerful, strutted. Through the glass,
Now lightly traced in frost, a mass
Of silver hid the trees and lay,
A gentle carpet, on the hill,
And all was white and clear and still.

2

Winter! The peasant in its honor
Marks out the roadway with his sleigh;
His poor horse plowing through the furrows
Goes jogging, stumbling, on its way.
And piling powdery ridges high
A swift kibitka dashes by,
The coachman in his sheepskin pelt
Upon the box, with scarlet belt.
A little peasant boy runs past;
His dog is riding in his sled
And he is harnessed there instead.
One finger's nipped—he's not downcast—
While at the window he can see
His mother gesture warningly.

3

Perhaps you do not like such pictures—
Indeed, they have but little chance
To please, they are so ordinary
And quite devoid of elegance.
Another poet, kindled by
The gods, knew how to glorify
The first pure snow and every phase
Of winter joys with lovely phrase.
He will enchant you with his sweet
And flaming poetry, I know—
Those secret sleigh-rides in the snow—
I shall not struggle to compete
With him, nor yet with you who paid
Your homage to the Finnish maid.

4

Tatyana with a soul all Russian
Delighted, without knowing why
She did so, in the Russian winter
And all its icy purity:
The hoarfrost sparkling in the sun,
The glittering snow flushed pink at dawn,
The sleighing and the revelry
The nights before Epiphany.
The servant girls, those evenings, came
To their young mistresses to tell
Their fortunes. (Here old rites were well
Observed.) Each year they were the same:
A military husband and
A journey coming, close at hand.

5

Tatyana trusted in the simple
Traditions of an older age
And she believed in cards and visions
And what the moon's face might presage.
She was disturbed by omens—she
Saw everywhere some mystery
Whose secret meanings would impart
A dim foreboding to her heart.
A tom-cat with his little paw
Would wash his face and primly purr
Upon the stove—a sign to her
Of visitors. And if she saw
The young moon's crescent on the left,
She trembled and grew pale, bereft

6

Of all her senses. And whenever
A shooting star flashed down the sky
Tatyana as she watched it crumble
Away in sparks would quickly try
While still she saw its rolling fire
To whisper out her heart's desire
In great excitement. If a hare
By chance should cross her path somewhere,
Or if she met a black-robed monk,
Not knowing what to do and quite
Beside herself with sudden fright
She stopped in horror and then shrunk
Away, while dread and fear would master
Her heart with warnings of disaster.

7

You laugh? But Tanya had discovered
The hidden joy in horror; we
Are all inclined indeed by nature
To lean towards incongruity.
Then Christmas came! Ah, what delight!
The young told fortunes day and night,
For youth has no regrets or fears;
Before it stretch the endless years,
All bright. And old age, peering through
Its spectacles, tells fortunes, though
It's near the grave and it must know
What's over no one can undo.
But what of that? False hope can still
Awake in all a childish thrill.

8

With eager eyes Tatyana watches
The candle dwindling more and more,
Its strangely molded pattern tells her
Of something marvelous in store.
Then rings are thrown into a bowl
And old refrains begin to roll
In chorus; Tanya takes her ring
And all the girls begin to sing:
"Oh, there the men are all so rich
They scoop up silver with a spade:
So fame and fortune to this maid."
But the refrain's complaining pitch
Foretold misfortune. Maidens found
The cat-song a more joyful sound.

9

A night of frost; the sky is shining;
The lovely galaxy of stars
Floats gently in the peaceful heavens—
And now Tatyana comes outdoors
In low-cut dress and softly turns
Her mirror to where Luna burns;
But in the dark and trembling glass
Only the moon's sad shadows pass.
Yet hush— a crackling— someone's there—
The girl runs forward on tiptoe,
Her faint voice ringing through the snow
More tender than the piper's air:
"What is your name?" The man looks on
And answers dully, "Agathon."

10

Tatyana, as her nurse has counseled,
Intends to read her fate this night;
She has them carry to the bath house
A table laid for two—but fright
Comes suddenly upon her. (So
I shiver at Svyetlana. No,
We neither one of us are bold
Enough to get our fortunes told.)
So lingeringly she unties
Her sash of silk and goes to bed
While Lel is hovering overhead,
But underneath her pillow lies
Her mirror, buried safe and deep.
Now all is still and she's asleep.

11

That night Tatyana dreamed of marvels.
She thought she was surrounded by
A gloomy mist where she was walking
Upon a meadowland piled high
With snowdrifts; and that on before
She heard a river foam and roar,
Its dark and whirling waters still
Ice-free in all the winter chill.
Two planks cemented by the ice
Were laid across the foaming stream,
A narrow bridge that well might seem
A risky span for that abyss.
So caught up by a sudden spasm
Of doubt she stopped before the chasm.

12

Tatyana fretted as if seeing
Some trifling check that might deter
Her progress, for she saw nobody
Beyond to reach a hand to her.
Then suddenly a snowdrift moved
And out from underneath it shoved
A huge and shaggy bear before
Her eyes. She gasped. He gave a roar
And offered her his sharp-clawed paw,
And trembling, almost fainting, she
Stretched out her hand reluctantly,
And falteringly let him draw
Her on across the stream. Once there
She kept on, followed by the bear.

13

Not daring once to turn she hurries,
But close behind her comes that shape;
Her tousled footman still attends her,
She cannot manage to escape.
The hateful bear with groans and sighs
Advances. Now a forest lies
Before them; stern and motionless
The pine trees stand, a heavy dress
Of snow upon their branches. Through
The barren tops of aspens, birches,
And lindens shine the night's bright torches,
But not a path or shrub in view—
The storm has buried all below
The heaped-up piles of mounded snow.

14

Tatyana races to the forest;
Her knees sink in the crumbling trough
Of snow. The bear comes stumbling after.
A branch has caught her and tears off
Her small gold earrings; one wet shoe
Sticks in the heavy snow; now too
Her handkerchief—she sees it drop
But in her terror dares not stop,
Hearing the bear come after her;
And yet she is ashamed to lift
Her skirts to help her through the drift
And make the walking easier.
She runs, he follows as before,
Till finally she can run no more.

15

She's fallen, and as quick as lightning
The bear has caught and lifted her;
Almost insensible, submissive,
She scarcely breathes and does not stir.
He bears her past the forest trees,
And suddenly ahead she sees
A tiny hut that had been placed
Deep in the snowy woodland waste.
But in the window is a light,
And noise and uproar sound within.
The bear speaks, "Inside is my kin,
He'll warm you at his house tonight."
With that he sets her down upon
The threshold and is straightway gone.

16

Tatyana breathes and looks around her.
She's on the porch—no bear at all.
Within are shouts and clinking glasses
As at some great man's funeral.
Just what it means she cannot think.
Then looking softly through a chink
She sees a table; circling it
All shapes and kinds of monsters sit:
One has a rooster's head, and one
The muzzle of a dog and horns;
She sees a goat's beard that adorns
A witch; a haughty skeleton,
A short-tailed dwarf, and something that
Is half a crane and half a cat.

17

It grows more strange and still more
    dreadful:
A crawfish 'strides a spider's back;
A skull in scarlet cape is whirling
Around upon a goose's neck.
A windmill dances Cossack-wise
With rattling wings; all over rise
Songs, laughter, horses' stamping—each
Gives vent to barks or human speech.
But what in heaven could it mean
When in that crew Tatyana saw
The one she loved and held in awe,
The hero of our verse, Eugene!
He sat at table with his glance
Directed toward the door, askance.

18

He makes a sign and all is motion,
He drinks and all must drink and shout,
He laughs and everyone laughs with him,
He frowns and all the cries die out.
For he is master, that is clear,
And Tanya feels a shade less fear
And, curious to gather more,
She pushes lightly on the door.
A gust of stormwind like a sheet
Blows out the lanterns, and the crowd
Of demons are disturbed and cowed.
Onegin rises from his seat,
And all the others do the same
While he comes on with eyes aflame.

19

Once more Tatyana is in terror
And tries to run; she cannot seem
To move, and though in wild impatience
She cannot fly, she cannot scream.
And now Eugene has pushed the door
And there Tatyana stands before
The eyes of all those fiends from hell.
She hears their crazy laughter swell
And burst, and every animal,
With hoofs and tusks and tufted tails,
Warped trunks and bloody tongues and
 nails,
Feelers and horns and fingers, all
Are pointing with a dreadful sign
And shrieking out, "She's mine, she's mine!"

20

"Mine!" cried Eugene with threatening
 gesture,
And suddenly the crowd was gone;
There in the frosty dusk Tatyana
And he were in the room alone.
Onegin seats her silently
Upon a shaky bench and he,
Sitting beside her, lays his head
Upon her shoulder, quieted.
Then Olga suddenly appears
With Lensky. Next a flash of light—
And now Onegin has his right
Arm lifted wildly as he jeers
His unasked guests and then lets loose
A feverish torrent of abuse.

21

Half swooning, Tanya hears the quarrel
Grow louder, sees Onegin lift
A dagger and sees Lensky prostrate.
Then dreadful shadows gathering swift
Blot out the light. The cottage shakes
And Tanya in her terror wakes...
The morning light has come again
And through the frosty window pane
A crimson glitter glows. The door
Bursts open. Olga, pinker than
Aurora's rosy caravan,
Light as a swallow, stands before
Her sister, asking, all delight,
"Whom did you dream about last night?"

22

Tatyana scarcely heard her sister
And gave her neither word nor look,
But lay in bed and turned the pages
In blind absorption of her book.
And though this book did not contain
A poet's fancies, sweet and vain,
Nor solemn truth nor pictured scene;
Yet neither Virgil nor Racine,
Byron nor Seneca nor Scott
Nor even the Ladies' Fashion Sheet
Could yield enchantment more complete
Than wise Martyn Zadeka, not
Surpassed by seers of any ages,
The master of Chaldean sages.

23

This most profound and treasured volume
Was brought into their solitude
One season by a wandering peddler.
Tatyana managed to conclude
A sale. For this and one more book,
Malvina, the old vendor took
Three rubles and a half, but had
Two grammars and a Petriad
Thrown in as weight to balance it,
With some old folk-tales, too, as well
As an odd book of Marmontel.
It soon was Tanya's favorite,
Her solace and her comforter,
And always went to bed with her.

24

The dream she'd had disturbed Tatyana;
She could not settle in her mind
Upon the true interpretation
Which she was so concerned to find.
She searched the index through where lay
In alphabetical array
Words such as forest, bear, and crow,
Hedgehog and fir tree, bridge and snow
And blizzard, yet her quandary
Martyn Zadeka had not solved
And she foresaw herself involved
Together with her family
In ominous events. Upset
For days, she still could not forget.

25

But now from out the morning valleys
The day has ushered in the sun
That is to light her festive name-day.
From dawn the house is overrun
With guests from all the neighborhood
Arriving with their numerous brood
In coach or sleigh or carryall.
There's anxious jostling in the hall
And greetings in the drawing room,
The barking of the little pug,
The younger girls who kiss and hug,
Laughter and noise as new guests come,
Bows, curtsies, and polite replies
And nurses' screams and childrens' cries.

26

Here with his buxom wife has driven
The round and portly Pustyakov;
Gvozdin, a splendid host, the owner
Of serfs all miserably off.
The two Skotinins, turning gray,
With children ranging all the way
From two to thirty years or so,
And Petyushkov the district beau.
There was my cousin too, Buyanov,
Unshaven in a vizored cap
(I think you know the careless chap),
And the ex-counselor, old Flyanov,
The rogue and gossip of the town,
A gluttonous, bribe-taking clown.

[121]

27

Monsieur Triquet was in the party
That came with Pamphil Karlikov,
A wit in auburn wig and glasses,
A late arrival from Tambov.
And he in truly Gallic way
Had brought a rhyme to grace the day
Set to the childhood melody,
Réveillez-vous, belle endormie.
Triquet had found it in the dust
Of an old almanac, and he,
Regardful of posterity,
Had thought as poet that he must
Preserve it; but for *belle Niná*
He said instead *belle Tatyaná*.

28

And finally there came the captain
Belonging to the post near by,
The idol of maturer damsels
On whom their mothers cast an eye
Of hope. What news he brings! They say
The regimental band will play!—
It is the colonel's own command.
What bliss! A ball! The young girls stand
Already trying their steps out. Then
The meal is served. Each couple goes
Out arm in arm, the girls in rows
Round Tanya, opposite the men.
All cross themselves—a buzzing meets
The ears, and so they take their seats.

29
The talking ceases for a little—
All mouths are busy. Everywhere
Are plates and knives and forks aclatter
And glasses clinking in the air.
But gradually all begin
To speak, and then a general din
Of laughter, shouts, and argument,
None listening, but all content.
Then suddenly the door swings wide
And Lensky enters with Eugene.
Old Madame Larin, who has seen
Them, cries, "At last!"—All push aside
Their chairs to make two places for
The friends now standing in the door.

30
They seat them opposite Tatyana;
She, trembling like a hunted deer
And paler than the moon at morning,
Can't lift her eyes grown dark with fear.
Her passion burns without restraint,
It stifles her and she grows faint.
She does not hear the words they say
In greeting. Tears have found their way
Into her eyes. Poor child! She might,
She thinks, at any minute swoon.
But will and reason conquer soon;
And so two words, with teeth clenched tight,
She somehow utters to each guest
And stays at table with the rest.

31

Displays of nerves and tragic gestures,
Young ladies' fainting-fits and tears,
Onegin hated: he had witnessed
Too many of them through the years.
Now, with his eccentricity,
Discovering himself to be
At such a crowded feast, he grew
Annoyed. When timid Tanya drew
Her eyes away, abashed, he frowned
And swore he'd drive Vladimir mad
To punish the officious lad.
Rejoicing in the scheme he'd found,
He started in his mind to draw
Burlesques of all the guests he saw.

32

Besides Eugene, the others present
Might well have seen the embarrassment
Of Tanya, but all eyes were viewing
A juicy pasty just then sent
To table (salted, though, almost
Too much), and then between the roast
And the blancmange they had brought in
Tsimlyanski wine from some dark bin,
And now a row of glasses tall
And slender as your little waist,
O Zizi, whom my youthful taste
Adored as something magical,
The crystal vial that fired me
To drunken, harmless poetry.

33

They draw the cork out, moist and swollen,
The bottle pops, the wine flows free.
And here, long tortured by his couplet,
Triquet arises solemnly
In front of all the gathering,
A silent and respectful ring.
Tatyana scarcely breathes; Triquet,
Holding his paper, turns her way
And sings, his voice not wholly true.
Applause and shouting greet him. Now
Tatyana in her turn must bow.
The poet, flushed but modest too,
Toasts her and then with gesture grand
He puts the verses in her hand.

34

Then came the name-day salutations;
Tatyana had to thank each one,
And when, confused, she reached Onegin
She looked so tired, so undone,
That an unwonted pity stirred
Within him and without a word
He bowed; but somehow he imbued
His look with real solicitude.
Now whether moved by her distress,
Or seeing in the circumstance
A call to flirt, or just by chance,
Or through some native kindliness,
His eyes were tender just the same:
They set Tatyana's heart aflame.

35

The chairs scrape back. The guests crowd
    into
The drawing room. Just so, concealed
Till then within the sugary beehive
Do bees swarm buzzing to the field.
Contented with the dinner that
They'd had, the neighbors sit and chat,
The ladies seek the fireplace,
The girls a more secluded space
To whisper in. Now they unfold
The green-topped tables. Modern whist
Calls up its votaries to assist,
Omber and boston claim the old,
A great monotonous family
All born of gluttonous ennui.

36

The knights of whist have played eight
    rubbers
By now, and eight times have they changed
Their places, and now tea is ready,
The service brought in and arranged.
I love to tell the time by tea,
By dinner, and by supper. We
Old country-dwellers like to say
Our stomach is the best Bréguet.
My verses are as full, or nearly,
Of different dishes, different wines,
Of what one drinks and how one dines
(All this I say in passing, merely)
As yours, great Homer, yours, which more
Than thirty centuries adore.

37

Yes, as to banquets I'm unyielding
And challenge your supremacy,
Though on some other points I freely
Confess that you have vanquished me:
Your heroes raging in their pride,
Your battles, if unjustified,
Your Cypris and your Zeus, outweigh
My cold Onegin any day,
Our dull and sleeping meadowland,
Istomina on whirling toe,
And all the fashionable show
Our education can command.
But Tanya's sweeter, that I swear,
Than wretched Helen, false though fair.

38

But we shan't quarrel over Helen
Though Menelaus should not cease
To waste poor Phrygia for another
Long hundred years for her release;
Though gathered round old Priam's throne
The ancient men of Pergamon
Beholding Helen, wondrous, bright,
Once more should judge both suitors right.
And as for combats, on that score
I beg you to be patient still
And not to judge too harshly till
You've read my book a little more.
A combat there shall surely be;
I swear to that, so trust in me.

39

But let's go on. With prim decorum
The girls have scarcely touched their tea
When through the doors to the long hallway
Bassoon and flute burst suddenly.
Delighted with the roar and hum,
Abandoning his tea and rum,
The local Paris, Petyushkov,
Comes up to carry Olga off.
Then Lensky and Tatyana, next
The poet from Tambov beside
The Karlikov, an ancient bride.
Our friend Buyanov has annexed
A Pustyakov. They crowd the hall—
It has begun, the glittering ball.

40

I wanted earlier in my story
To paint for you (see Canto One)
St. Petersburg's resplendent ballrooms
As an Albani might have done.
But I was led astray by sweet
Vain dreams of all the little feet
Of ladies whom I used to know;
Now it is time I ceased to go
Along their slender trail and I'll
Restrain myself, since I am through
With youth, and make an effort to
Improve my business and my style
And keep this present canto clear
Of wanderings which should not appear.

41

Monotonous yet wild like any
Young life that longs to soar and fly,
The waltzers hum and spin as couple
On couple flashes swiftly by.
Onegin, smiling secretly,
Approaches Olga. He can see
His vengeance nearing. Now he's bowed
And they are circling through the crowd.
He finds a chair for her and then
Begins a confidential chat,
And just a minute after that
He starts to waltz with her again.
The ballroom watches in surprise,
While Lensky cannot trust his eyes.

42

Then came the sound of the mazurka.
In olden days its thunderous roar
Made all the vast hall shake and boot heels
Roused creakings from the inlaid floor,
While every window in its frame
Went rattling. Now we've grown more tame
And on the polished boards we glide
Like ladies. But the countryside
Is different. The mazurka's kept
Its figures fresh and natural,
Moustaches, leaping, heels and all,
And nothing in it has been swept
Away by the harsh fashion that
Is modern Russia's autocrat.

43

Just as the whip drives haughty fillies
On tether round the riding ring,
So do the men direct their partners
In dizzy rounds to whirl and swing.
Our Petyushkov will split the floor
(The old retired counselor)
In boots and spurs. Buyanov too
Goes stamping, plowing stoutly through.
But now the youths set to, with shout
And crash and furious din and whiz
And trampling: the *prisyadka* is
The only turn that they leave out.
But gentler, gentler! or, who knows,
Those heels will crush some lady's toes!

44

The wild Buyanov brings Tatyana
And Olga to Onegin. He
Walks off at once with Olga. Lightly
He leads her, gliding easily,
And whispers softly, bending near,
Some foolish verses in her ear,
Pressing her hand. Her pink face glows
With pleasure to a deeper rose.
Poor Lensky's witnessed all that passed;
In jealous rage he turns a bright
Indignant scarlet at the sight
And when the dance is through at last
He asks for the cotillion if
She's free, his manner cold and stiff.

45

But Olga cannot give it him.
Why not? It's promised to Eugene.
Onegin! Oh, dear Lord in Heaven,
What does he hear? What can it mean?
She hardly out of bibs, and yet
This heedless child a vain coquette,
Already practiced in deceit,
A trickster and a foolish cheat!
Young Lensky cannot bear this blow,
And cursing soundly all the course
Of women's wiles, he gets his horse
And gallops off abruptly. No,
Two pistols, nothing else, must be
His arbiters of destiny.

Canto SIX

*Là, sotto giorni nubilosi e brevi,
Nasce una gente a cui 'l morir
non dole.*

—PETRARCH.

1

O<small>N SEEING</small> Lensky leave, Onegin
Sat bored and mute at Olga's side
But still content to all appearance
With the revenge that he had tried;
While Olga yawned in company
And looked for Lensky fruitlessly
And the cotillion seemed as long
As some bad dream where all goes wrong.
But it has ended—supper comes;
The guests are tired; and for each
A bed is made. The quarters reach
From entrance hall to servants' rooms.
Onegin is the only one
To leave, and he rides off alone.

2

Now all were quiet. Fat and portly,
Both Pustyakovs lay snoring in
The drawing room, and our Buyanov
With Petyushkov and with Gvozdin
On chairs, were in the dining hall
With Flyanov, not himself at all,
And on the floor Monsieur Triquet
In undervest and nightcap lay.
In Olga's and Tatyana's rooms
The girls were sound asleep; and there,
Beside the window, sad and fair,
Diana's pallid light illumes
Poor Tanya sitting in the dark
And gazing out upon the park.

3

Onegin's unexpected visit,
His momentary tender gaze,
His curious attitude to Olga,
Had left her in a helpless daze
And wounded her profoundly. She
Was torn by pangs of jealousy.
It was as though an icy hand
Had gripped her heart; as though the land
Had opened in a roaring lake
Of blackness underneath her. "I
Shall perish," Tanya said, "but why
Should I not perish for his sake?
I don't complain. It's sweeter so.
He could not love me; that I know."

4

But still another person clamors
For our attention—let's make haste.
Five miles away from Krasnogorye
And Lensky's village, in the waste,
Like true philosopher, lived one
Zaretsky. In his time he'd run
The gamut—tribune of the inns
And gamblers' chieftain—all the sins
In vogue he'd tried; but in the end
He'd turned a peaceful squire, good
And simple, with a growing brood,
Though still unmarried. A true friend
And honest man. One must allow
We do improve with age, somehow.

5

In former days the world had flattered
His daring with a generous flow
Of praise; for he could shoot an ace-spot
From thirty feet away or so.
And then upon another score
He was distinguished; in the war,
Dead drunk, he rode his Kalmuk horse
One day a frantic muddy course
Till captured by the French, a pawn
Most precious! Yet this perilous
Ordeal our modern Regulus
Would once again have undergone
If every day at Véry's still
On credit he might drink his fill.

6

He had been famous for his hoaxing
Of fools, and he would mortify
The clever, too, by skillful banter
Quite openly or on the sly;
Although sometimes his trickery
Had cost him very dear and he
Had got into an awful hole
Exactly like a simpler soul.
He could debate in cheerful fashion,
Make witty or obtuse replies,
Be silent when that seemed more wise
Or argue with judicious passion
And make young friends fall out and bring
Them on at last to dueling;

7

Or else he'd smooth their quarrel over
And they would go to lunch, all three,
And when the two had left he'd slur them
With slanders uttered wittily.
Sed alia tempora! It seems
That daring, like a lover's dreams
(Another folly), goes with youth;
And my Zaretsky was in truth
Sheltered at last from storms, a sage
Who planted cabbages and praised
The chickens and the geese he raised,
Like Horace in another age.
And there beneath his locust trees
He taught his young their A B C's.

8

He was not stupid. Though Onegin
Could not esteem his heart, yet that
Did not prevent him from enjoying
His sensible and clever chat.
He used to like to have him call
And so was not surprised at all
Next morning when the man rode in.
Zaretsky, though, did not begin
The easy talk he could command,
But with a glance amused and keen
Delivered over to Eugene
A letter in the poet's hand,
And this Onegin, moving toward
The window, read without a word.

9
It was both dignified and civil,
Arriving briefly at its end:
With cold, polite decision Lensky
Had sent a challenge to his friend.
Onegin did not hesitate
In just as simple words to state
His answer: he was quite prepared
At any moment, he declared.
Zaretsky rose and closed the scene.
He did not wish for more delay,
He still had much to do that day
And left for home at once. Eugene,
A prey to thought, the envoy gone,
Was ill content with what he'd done.

10
And, judging strictly, with good reason!
He called himself to stern account:
He had been wrong in the beginning—
He saw the list of charges mount—
To play last night so carelessly
With love that was so sweet and shy.
And Lensky, in the second place,
Might be allowed a little grace—
A boy he loved and just eighteen!
Yes, it was he who was amiss
To show himself all prejudice
To one so ardent—he, Eugene,
A man of honor and of sense,
No hotspur quick to take offense.

11

He could have shown the boy his feelings
And not have bristled like a beast;
He should have spoken some disarming
Reply, he thought. "But now, at least,
It's far too late; the time has gone
And this old duelist's been drawn
Completely into the affair,
A wicked gossip with a flair
For talking. One of course detests
And ought to scorn his jeers; but then,
The mocking words of foolish men..."
On just such social thinking rests
That honor which we all revere,
The very axis of our sphere.

12

At home the poet waits the outcome,
Impatient, hot with enmity,
Till finally his loquacious neighbor
Brings him his answer solemnly.
The jealous man is now content:
He feared Eugene, on mischief bent,
Might somehow by some clever ruse
Retreat and, offering some excuse,
Avert the bullet from his heart.
But now his doubts are gone. They will
Both meet tomorrow at the mill
At daybreak, each to act his part,
To raise the trigger and take aim
At leg or brow, to kill or maim.

13
Vladimir, sure he hates his Olga
Henceforward, and resolved to shun
The cold coquette before the duel,
Takes out his watch, surveys the sun,
Is tempted, and capitulates—
And here he's at his neighbor's gates.
He thought his coming would appal
And startle Olga. Not at all!
From off the porch on flying feet
Ran Olinka, her playful ways
Exactly as on other days,
Her smile of greeting just as sweet,
Like hope the fickle, free from care,
And gay and bright and debonair.

14
"Why did you go away so early
Last night?" were the first words she said.
Vladimir grew confused, he faltered,
And without answering bent his head.
His jealous anger could not blaze
Beneath this clear and candid gaze,
Before this sweet simplicity,
This blithe and joyful spirit. He
Beholds her face with rapture, for
He is convinced she loves him still;
And now remorse and sorrow fill
His heart and, ready to implore
Forgiveness, and yet reassured,
He trembles. He is almost cured.

15, 16, 17

But now Vladimir, downcast, wistful,
With charming Olga in his sight,
Has not the power to remind her
Of all that had occurred last night.
He reasons: "I will come between
And save her from that libertine,
Who with his sighs and flattery
Would tempt her heart away from me.
Shall the vile, venomous worm be let
To gnaw the lily's stem and kill
The blossoms of two mornings, still
A-bud and not all opened yet?"
Which means, dear readers, in the end:
"I'll fight this duel with my friend."

18

Had Lensky known about Tatyana
And of the wound that scorched her heart:
Had she conjectured what was coming,
Or been informed by any art
That Lensky and Eugene would brave
At dawn the shadow of the grave,
Her love, perhaps, might even then
Have reconciled the friends again,
But of her passion no one guessed.
Onegin had kept silent, she
Had wept her sorrow secretly
Nor had chance made it manifest.
Her nurse might have suspected it,
But she was far too dull of wit.

19

Lensky looked absent all the evening,
Now silent and now swiftly gay;
But one who is the muses' nursling
Is always so. He'd start to play
The clavichord, but then he frowned
And only single bars would sound.
And he would say to Olga, low:
"Ah, am I happy? Is it so?"
But it is time to leave. His heart
So pained him as he said goodbye
To Olga with a lingering sigh
That it was almost torn apart.
"Is something wrong, then?" Olga cried.
"No, nothing," and he's gone outside.

20

At home he looked his pistols over
And put them back into the case,
Undressed, and by the candle's glimmer
He opened Schiller. But one face,
One thought have power over him,
And everything on earth is dim
But Olga, whom his sad thoughts dress
In a surpassing loveliness.
Vladimir shuts the book and takes
His pen; the verses full and free
Pour out in love's fond ecstasy
Until the lyric fever shakes
His soul and he recites his lines
Like drunken Delvig when he dines.

21

It happens that we have his verses,
And I present them to your gaze:
Oh, whither, whither have you vanished,
Dear springtime of my golden days?
What does the future hold for me?
I struggle but in vain to see;
The dark envelops all; nor need
One know, for fate is just indeed.
And if the arrow pierce me through
Or pass me, and I'm left unharmed,
Yet all is good. The hour is charmed
That strikes for sleep and waking, too.
So blest the day of toil, and blest
The fall of night when all shall rest.

22

Aurora will be bright at morning,
Another sparkling day will come,
And I, perhaps, shall be descending
To the dark secrets of the tomb,
And Lethe's sluggish tide will drown
Another poet's young renown.
The world will then forget—but you,
O maiden beautiful and true,
Will you not weep me where I lie,
And think,"I was his very own
And he had vowed to me alone
His stormy youth, so soon to die!"
My love, oh, hasten to my side,
The friend I long for, you, my bride!

23

So Lensky wrote: vague, weak expressions
(Such are romanticism's flowers,
Though why romantic I can't gather—
But still, that's no concern of ours).
Then finally just before the red
Of dawn he let his tired head
Droop down above that modern word,
"Ideal," and no longer stirred.
But as his dreams began to make
Fair visions round him, in there came
His silent friend, who called his name
And summoned Lensky to awake:
"High time to rise, it's seven almost;
Onegin will be at his post."

24

But he was wrong in that: Onegin
Was sound asleep. The shadows grow
More thin as night retreats and Vesper
Is greeted by the rooster's crow,
And still Onegin sleeps. The sun
Has long since risen and begun
Its course, and now in gleaming curls
A passing snowstorm beats and whirls.
And still he sleeps and still the wide
Soft wings of slumber guard his bed
Until at last he lifts his head
And pulls the curtain-folds aside.
He looks around; it's time indeed
To leave the house, and that with speed.

25

He rings in haste, until his servant
Comes running in, the French Guillot,
To bring his dressing gown and slippers
And hand his clothes to him. And so
Onegin dresses hurriedly
And tells his servant he must be
Prepared likewise to come, and place
The pistols by him in their case.
The sleighs are ready, and, afraid
To wait, he's off. Arriving there,
He tells his serving man to bear
The fatal arms Le Page had made
And follow him; the sleighs must stand
Off farther in the meadowland.

26

Meanwhile impatient Lensky, leaning
Upon the dam, was forced to hear
Zaretsky's lecture on the millstone
In rôle of village engineer.
Onegin first apologized.
"But," said Zaretsky in surprised
Response, "your second, where is he?"
For, of a classic pedantry
In duels, he would not depart
From rule. To stretch a man out you
Must do it all according to
The strictest canons of the art
In all the old traditional ways
(For which he well deserves our praise).

27

"My second?" said Eugene in answer,
"Why here, my friend, Monsieur Guillot.
I think you'll hardly make objections
To being introduced. Although
He's not illustrious, he's throughout
An honest man, beyond a doubt."
Zaretsky bit his lip; and then
Onegin turned to Lensky,"When
Shall we begin?" "Why, now, I think,"
Vladimir answered, and the two
Walked off while with so much to do
Zaretsky and the valet sink
Into discussion most profound;
The foes stand looking at the ground.

28

And yet how long had they been strangers
Athirst for one another's blood?
How long, since they had shared their
    leisure
As friends, their thoughts and acts, their
    food?
And now in fury they propose,
As two hereditary foes
In some wild nightmare dream might do,
Cold-bloodedly, in silence, to
Destroy each other. Had they not
Far better laugh and let it go
Before the blood begins to flow,
And part in peace without a shot?
But quarrels of society
Fear false dishonor horribly.

29

The metal of the pistols flashes,
The hammers clang, and down inside
The rifled barrels with their facets
The bullets ominously slide.
The triggers click, and in what seems
Two slowly moving grayish streams
The powder fills the pans, and then
The locks, screwed in, are fixed again.
Behind a stump Guillot, perplexed,
Looks as Zaretsky measures there
Some thirty steps with gravest care.
The rivals drop their cloaks and next
They're stationed on their lines and stand
Each with a pistol in his hand.

30

"Advance!" Remorseless, not yet raising
His pistol to take aim, each foe
Came on four even steady paces,
Four deadly steps, unhurried, slow.
Onegin was the first to lift
His weapon and without a shift
Of time walked forward five steps more
Unhesitating as before,
While Lensky, screwing up one eye
As better marksmanship required,
Took aim. But then Onegin fired—
The poet's day was past and by,
His hour had struck. Without a sound
His pistol dropped upon the ground.

31

His hand goes gently to his bosom.
He falls. His eyes, grown dim and wide,
Are eloquent of death, not anguish.
So slowly down the mountainside,
Shining and sparkling in the sun,
An avalanche of snow rolls on.
Onegin in a sudden chill
Runs toward the boy, who lies quite still.
He looks at him and calls. No power
Can wake him now; his youthful friend
Has come to a too early end.
The storm has breathed, the morning flower
Has withered, blasted in the rout,
The altar fire has flickered out.

32

He lay unmoving. On his forehead
A strange and lifeless peace had spread;
His breast was pierced through by the bullet,
And blood still trickled, hot and red.
A moment since and in this heart
Ecstatic dreams were used to start
And hope and love and seething hate
And life were wont to congregate.
But as a house deserted might,
It gives no sound and never will
And all is dark and very still,
With windows whitewashed, shutters tight,
And hostess gone; nor does a trace
Remain to tell her dwelling place.

33

It's pleasant with a brazen sally
To infuriate a careless foe
And watch him obstinately lower
His threatening horns against the blow
And see him shamed if he shall pass
His likeness in the looking glass;
And still more pleasant if he cry
In sheer stupidity, "It's I."
And even pleasanter to plan
His honorable grave and from
The proper distance, cool and dumb,
To aim unshaken at your man.
And yet to send him off to join
His ancestors is not so fine.

34

Suppose the bullet from your pistol
Has shot to death a youthful friend
Who with some word or indiscretion
Or trifle managed to offend
Your feelings as you chanced to share
A bottle; or suppose some flare
Of anger makes him proudly call
You out. What awful dread will fall
Upon your heart when you behold
Him fallen on the ground with death
Upon his brow, no stir of breath,
And see him stiffen and grow cold;
When he is deaf and dumb to all
The words that you so wildly call.

35

In passionate remorse, still clutching
The pistol in his hand with dread,
Eugene stood looking at Vladimir.
"So, then," Zaretsky said, "he's dead."
He's dead! And crushed by a decree
So awful, mutely, shudderingly,
Eugene walked off and called his men.
With all due care Zaretsky then
Arranged the body on the sleigh
To carry back the dreadful load.
Scenting a corpse, the horses pawed
And snorted, mad to be away,
And champed their bits now white with foam,
Then flew as swift as arrows home.

36

My friends, you mourn a poet dying,
His hopes, like flowers, not yet full-blown,
With nothing in the world accomplished,
The clothes of childhood just outgrown.
For where are now the burning fire,
The yearning, and the young desire,
The thoughts and passions manifold,
Lofty and gentle and yet bold?
Where are the cravings after love,
The eagerness to work and know,
The dread of shame and all things low,
The visions of a life above
The earthly one that we can see,
The dreams of sacred poetry?

37

Perhaps he would have been a blessing
To all mankind, or won renown;
Perhaps his lyre so early silenced
Would have gone ringing loudly down
The years. He might have lived to be
The darling of society.
It may be that his martyred ghost
Took with it, now forever lost
To us, a sacred mystery.
And he is gone beyond recall
With his life-giving voice; and all
The praises of posterity
Can never reach to that far place
To bear the blessings of the race.

38, 39

And then again perhaps the poet
Would have enjoyed a simple lot.
His youth would go and with its passing
His ardor would have grown less hot.
He would have changed in many ways
And lived his happy married days,
The muses gone, away from town,
A cuckold in a dressing gown.
He would have known reality,
By forty have acquired gout,
Have eaten, drunk, and gotten stout,
And round his deathbed he would see
His children and the doctors crowd
While all the women wept aloud.

40

Alas, whatever might have happened,
The youthful lover met his end;
The poet and the wistful dreamer
Became the victim of his friend.
There is a spot not far from where
The muses' nursling lived, and there
Two pines, their roots united, grow.
A little brook winds on below
And goes to join a near-by stream.
There often some poor laborer will
Find rest, and peasant women fill
Their clinking jugs that flash and gleam.
And near the brook a simple stone
Is set in shadow, all alone.

41

Beneath it when the first spring showers
Have touched the fields, and winter's past,
The shepherd sings of Volga fishers
And weaves himself his shoes of bast.
And when the young girl, city-bred,
Who spends her summers here has fled
Alone on horseback, galloping
Across the fields, she'll often bring
Her filly up before this stone.
Drawing her reins in, with her veil
Thrown back, she reads the simple tale
That's written on a grave unknown.
She gazes pensively and sighs
And gentle tears then fill her eyes.

42

She rides more slowly through the country
Far lost in revery, her mind
Completely taken up with Lensky
And fate so cruel and unkind.
And then she thinks of Olga: "Did
She weep for long or was she rid
Of sorrow very soon? And how
Is she, the other sister, now?
And he, the gloomy enemy
Who shuns the world in which he dwells,
The modern foe of modern belles,
The poet's murderer, where is he?"
Some day I'll tell you all about
These things, with not a word left out.

43

But not just now, although my hero
Has always had my real regard
And though I'll tell you of him later.
I have no time at present. Hard,
Stern prose has claimed me. Age and time
Both tend to banish teasing rhyme,
And though I sigh that this should be
I now pursue her lazily.
No longer does my pen-point race
Across the paper, scrawling there
My dreams, but cooler, sterner care
Has come upon me now to chase
My peaceful visions far from me
In solitude or company.

44

For other aspirations call me,
With other sorrow I am filled,
Although I have no expectations
And my old grief is not yet stilled.
Where is your sweetness gone, old dreams?
And where is youth that always seems
Your fitting rhyme? And is youth's crown
Already wilted, dry and brown?
And is it really true at last
That, elegiac phrase aside,
My springtime days have really died
As I said joking in the past?
Were they so soon to disappear?
Can I be in my thirtieth year?

45

Yes, afternoon has come upon me,
I must acknowledge it, I know,
And say farewell in friendly fashion
To youth and all its buoyant show.
I thank you for your joys and for
Your torments, sad and sweet, once more,
And for the feasts and jollity
And tumult that you brought to me.
For I enjoyed them, every phase
Of that existence had its charms,
Whether in peace or wild alarms;
But they are over now, those days,
And with an undivided mind
I start anew, youth left behind.

46

But let me look around at parting:
Halls of my quiet life, farewell!
Days filled with idleness and passion
And melancholy's gloomy spell!
And you, young heat and early fire,
Imagination and desire,
Fly to this quiet spot and stir
My sleeping spirit oftener.
Do not allow a poet's heart
To cool and harden slowly till
In this mad world that seeks to kill
All trace of spirit, every part
Is stone, there in the glittering press
Of haughty fools and soullessness;

47

Among crackbrained and pampered
    children,
Smallminded men with wily ways,
Ridiculous and boring wretches
And judges captious with dispraise;
Among coquettes of pious mien
And every fashionable scene
Of daily life—servility,
Polite and flattering treachery,
Censorious, stupid judgments and
The most vexatious emptiness,
With scheming words and pitiless
Frivolities on every hand—
In short, dear readers, in the slough
Where you and I are rolling now.

Canto SEVEN

*O Moscow, Russia's favorite
daughter, Where shall we look
to find thy like?* —DMITRIEV.

*Our own, our Moscow, who
could fail to love thee?*

—BARATYNSKY.

*"Just hear the sneering traveler!
Where's a better spot
Than our own Moscow?"—
"Where we're not."*

—GRIBOYEDOV.

1

Now DRIVEN by the sun of springtime
From off the neighboring hills, the snow
Runs sweeping down in muddy rivers
To flood the meadows far below,
And nature, sleepy, smiling, clear,
Salutes the morning of the year.
The sky is dark with shimmering blue,
And one can still see clearly through
The woods, just touched with greening down;
The bee has left its waxy cell
To stock anew its citadel,
The motley fields no longer drown;
The cattle low, the nightingale
Already wakes the silent vale.

2

How sorrowful to me your coming,
O season made for love, O Spring!
What vague excitement fills my spirit
And makes my blood go hurrying!
When in some quiet country place
Quite suddenly across my face
The breath of spring begins to steal,
How poignant the delight I feel!
Will no such pleasures come again?
Will all things fresh and bright and glad,
All things triumphant, only add
More boredom to my heart, and pain?
And to my spirit, long since dead,
Must everything be filled with dread?

3

Perhaps we do not see with gladness
The leaves returning springs restore,
Because with each new forest-murmur
Old losses rise in us once more;
And when we see that nature wakes
Again, our puzzled thinking makes
The contrast to our dying years
With no rebirth as springtime nears.
Or in some poet's revery
Perhaps some long-past spring will rise
Again in dreams before our eyes
And in its thrilling light we see
A distant country, fair and bright,
A wonder-moon, a magic night.

4

Such is the season. Kindly idlers,
And sages, epicures in taste,
You fledglings of the school of Levshin,
You free and happy men, make haste!
You Priams of the soil, and you,
Dear sentimental ladies, too,
The spring has called you to the land,
The flowers are out, the sun is bland.
It is the time for walks inspired,
For all that tempting nighttime yields,
So hurry, hurry to the fields!
In heavy coach or ancient hired
Barouche and posthorse they've begun
To leave the city one by one.

5

And likewise you, indulgent reader,
In your own special foreign coach
Come, leave the busy town of winter
Delights, and hail the spring's approach.
Come with my wayward Muse and move
Beneath the softly rustling grove
Along the nameless river, in
The country where Eugene had been
Last winter's idle, sad recluse.
Come to the little village where
My own Tatyana, young and fair,
In gentle dreams was wont to muse.
But he has gone, and we shall find
Only the grief he left behind.

6

There is a meadow half surrounded
By hills, and there, slow journeying,
A little brook flows toward the river
Past banks where linden branches swing.
And there spring's love, the nightingale,
Sings all night long, and pink and frail
The briar blooms, and there beside
The stream two ancient pine trees hide
A tombstone; with an indrawn breath
The stranger reads its simple flow:
Vladimir Lensky lies below,
Who early died a valiant death
At such an age, in such a year.
Young poet, sleep untroubled here!

7

There where the pine trees bent their
    branches
The morning breezes used to toss
Above the quiet grave in secret
The plaited wreath that marks a loss.
And here two girls would often come
At night and, sitting on the tomb,
On which the moon poured down its light,
They wept and held each other tight.
But that is over, and the way
They passed so often vanished now.
There is no wreath upon the bough;
Only the shepherd, bent and gray,
Sings at its foot as long before,
Weaving his humble shoes once more.

8, 9, 10

Poor Lensky! No, she did not weep you
For very long nor waste away;
Your youthful bride was not too faithful,
Her sorrow did not come to stay.
For even now another fills
Her mind, another now instills
Into her soul a lover's balm.
It is an uhlan thus could calm
Her heart and whom she loves again;
And now before the altar she
Is standing, bending bashfully
Her downcast head, and even then
Her eyes are lit with fire while
Her lips are parted in a smile.

11

Poor Lensky! In those distant stretches
Of limitless eternity
Were you, sad singer, shocked at learning
The fatal news of treachery?
Or, lulled in blissful ignorance
On Lethe's shore, can no mischance
In regions hidden from your eyes
Now cause you horror or surprise?
Yes, deaf oblivion will await
Us all beyond the grave; no sound
From foes or sweethearts but is drowned
In silence. Only his estate
Provokes the chorusing of heirs
To hateful wrangling for their shares.

12

Now in the Larin household Olga
No longer sang in young content;
Her uhlan, victim of his calling,
Was ordered to his regiment.
Old Madame Larin needs must cry
On bidding her dear child goodbye,
Almost beside herself with grief.
But Tanya could not find relief
In tears, though on her pensive face
A deeper pallor spread when she
Came out upon the porch to see
Them off, while all the bustling place
Was filled with servants, come to tell
The newly married pair farewell.

13

She watches long with clouded vision
Until the carriage disappears,
And then she is alone: Tatyana
Has lost the friend of all these years!
Her little darling one, her dove,
Her only confidante, her love,
Is carried far away by fate
And their two lives must separate.
And as a shadow might, on feet
As still, she wanders aimlessly
Down empty garden paths, where she
Finds nothing any longer sweet.
Her stifled tears will not burst through;
Her heart is almost torn in two.

14

But in her loneliness her passion
Has not decreased but grown more strong
And from her mind the lost Onegin
Is never absent very long.
She cannot see him, and she ought
To hate and shun the very thought
Of one who killed a brother; yet
They all have managed to forget . . .
Has not the poet's own true love
Already found another one?
All thought of him is passed and gone
Like smoke into the blue above.
Only two hearts still grieve for him:
Why should his memory not grow dim?

15

It was at dusk. The sky had darkened,
The beetles buzzed, the river flowed
More calmly, and the peasants' dances
Were almost done. A fire glowed
Across the river through the smoke,
Just lighted by some fisher folk.
Then in the moonlit fields alone
Tatyana wandered on and on
Till all at once she saw the gleam
Of manor windows down below
The hill she stood on, and a row
Of trees, a garden, and a stream.
She looked and with a sudden start
She felt a pounding in her heart.

16

At first she stood in indecision—
"Shall I turn back or still go on?
I'd like to see the house and garden
And no one knows me—he is gone."
So almost breathless she descends
To the deserted yard and spends
A minute gazing helplessly
Till, scenting stranger company,
The dogs rush out at her and bark.
And then on hearing Tanya's cry
Of fright, the servant's boys near by
Run up to stop it and embark
Upon a war with great expense
Of shouts and noise, in her defense.

17

"I'd like to see the house," said Tanya,
"May I?" The children all once more
 Went running off to fetch Anisya
 And get the key to the front door.
 Anisya came and with a stir
 Unlocked the entrance hall for her,
 And Tanya found herself within
 The house where her Eugene had been
 So recently. She looked around:
 A billiard cue with rubber tip
 Forgotten on the board, a whip
 Thrown on the couch was what she found.
 And then the fireplace was shown
 Where the young master sat alone.

18

"Here in the winter," said Anisya,
"Our neighbor came to dine, now dead,
 And if you'll follow me I'll show you
 The study where he sat and read.
 He had his coffee here and slept,
 And saw the books the bailiff kept.
 My former master lived here, too;
 On Sundays when the week was through
 He'd put his glasses on and sit
 Beside the window there and play
 Old maid with me to pass away
 The time. God save him from the pit!
 And may damp Mother Earth not cease
 To guard his bones in rest and peace!"

19

With eyes that shone with love Tatyana
Looked all about her. Everything
She saw to her was something precious
And eased her heart of suffering.
She greeted with a touching smile
The table lamp beside the pile
Of books, the rug upon the bed
Beneath the window, where a thread
Of moonlight lit the outside scene;
Within, the quiet twilight and
Lord Byron's portrait and a stand
With a small iron figurine
With hat on, forehead dark, oppressed,
And arms tight-folded on his breast.

20

Here in this modern cell Tatyana
Was bound by magic long and deep.
But it grew late, the wind was colder,
The valley dark, the woods asleep
Above the misty stream. The moon
Had dropped behind the hill and soon
So young a pilgrim ought to start
For home. Tatyana must depart.
And so although it was a task
To overcome her tears, she tried
To conquer them and only sighed.
But she did not forget to ask
To visit this forlorn demesne
Again and read the books she'd seen.

21

She took her leave of the old woman
Outside the gate and went away,
But two days later, in the morning,
She came to make a longer stay,
And in the empty study where
No sound disturbed the silent air
She sat alone at last and cried,
Forgetting all the world outside.
But then the books engaged her; she
Discovered a selection strange
And quite beyond her usual range,
But as she read on avidly
She found herself caught up and hurled
Into another, alien world.

22

Onegin, as you will remember,
A little while ago began
To hate all reading; yet some volumes
He had excepted from this ban.
Such were *Don Juan* and *The Giaour*
And those few novels of the hour
In which he saw the times portrayed
With a degree of truth, that made
The modern man appear a cold
And selfish being with a quite
Immoral soul, a man who might
Possess illusions manifold,
His harsh, embittered mind a sea
That boiled with vain activity.

23

There still remained on many pages
The impress of a sharpened nail,
And all such marks the quick attention
Of Tanya noted without fail.
And quivering in every nerve
She was on fire to observe
What thoughts had struck Eugene and what
He acquiesced in or did not.
She found the margins often lined
With scribbled pencil marks that he
Had made. Involuntarily
And everywhere Onegin's mind
Unrolled itself before her gaze
Through question-mark or cross or phrase.

24

And now Tatyana, thanks to Heaven,
Began to grasp by slow degrees
The mind of him whom fate had destined
By its immutable decrees
She was to love. This strange and sad
And dangerous apparition, had
He come from Heaven or from Hell,
Angel or fiend—or empty shell?
Was he, when all was said and done,
The echo of a foreign air,
A Muscovite who wished to wear
Childe Harold's cloak, a lexicon
Of every fashionable rage—
A parody upon his age?

25

Did Tanya really solve the riddle
And did she find the magic key?
The hours ran on—she had forgotten
Her home and waiting family,
Where even now her mother sat
Confiding to some neighbors that
She had no notion what to do.
"She's not a child. Why, of the two
Our Olga was the younger. Yes,
It's time she settled down. But then,
How can I get her married when
She answers everyone's address
With 'No'? And then besides she's grown
So sad, and walks all day alone."

26

"Is she in love?"—"With whom? Buyanov
Proposed to her but was refused,
And Petyushkov. We had a visit
From the hussar Pykhtin. He used
His utmost powers. How he did rave
About our Tanya! Like a slave!
I thought perhaps she would consent—
But no, so finally off he went."—
"Then, my dear lady, take your charge
To Moscow. That's the market place
For brides. There's room, in any case."—
"Oh, but my income's not so large."—
"One winter and you should succeed.
If not, I'll lend you what you need."

27

Old Madame Larin was delighted
With this advice, both wise and kind,
And so she reckoned up expenses
And very soon made up her mind
To go. Then Tanya heard the news.
To face the world's exacting views,
To show her country artlessness,
Her long-outmoded style of dress
And simple features! To expose
Her speech, old-fashioned in their ears,
To the sophisticated sneers
Of Moscow Circes, Moscow beaux!
What horror! How much better, could
She linger in her own deep wood!

28

She rose as soon as it was morning
And hurried to the fields to look
With tender eyes upon their beauty,
And as she gazed she sadly took
A last farewell. "Calm valleys, high,
Familiar peaks and hills, goodbye!
And you, dear wood and hollow dell
All heavenly loveliness, farewell!
O happy Nature, I must leave
The quiet world where now I am
For brilliance and for empty sham,
A life I barely can conceive.
For I shall walk alone no more!
Oh, what does fortune hold in store!"

29

Each day Tatyana's walks were longer
As here a brook and there a knoll
Involuntarily detained her
And charmed her to her inmost soul;
As if they were old friends she'd met
She'd stay a little longer yet
In converse with her fields and groves.
But ever swiftly summer moves
And yellow fall is there instead,
And Nature, pale and trembling, stands
A sacrifice in golden bands.
The cold wind roars and drives ahead
The clouds, till Winter shall step forth,
The cold enchantress of the north.

30

She came and spread through wood and valley,
She hung in tufts upon the oaks,
She lay upon the hills and meadows
In carpets and in billowy cloaks.
She leveled banks and stream and spilt
Upon them both a downy quilt.
The frost shone white. We love to see
How Winter works her fantasy,
But Tanya grieves. She does not go
Outside to breathe the sparkling air
And from the bath-house porch prepare
To wash her neck and face with snow
And feel its tingling sting and nip:
Tatyana dreads the winter trip.

31

At last the day of the departure
Has come, postponed and overdue.
The old forgotten sleigh, gone over,
Upholstered and repaired anew,
Came out; the usual three sleighs more
Were heaped with an enormous store
Of household goods, trunks, saucepans,
    chairs,
Thick mattresses, preserves in jars,
A feather bed and pots and pails
And crates of roosters: every sort
Of thing that travelers need, in short.
The servants raise their farewell wails
Within the house to show regard
And eighteen horses crowd the yard.

32

The boyar coach is ready-harnessed,
The cooks bring out the lunch, and all
The three kibitkas are full-loaded,
The women and the coachmen brawl.
A bearded postboy sits astride
A nag whose bones push through its side,
The servants crowd the gate and cry
And bid their mistresses goodbye.
They're ready, and the ancient coach
Goes slipping, crawling, through the gate.
"Goodbye, dear land, so intimate,
Dear house no other can approach.
Shall I return?" It disappears,
And Tanya sheds a stream of tears.

33

When we give access to the blessings
That civilized conditions bring
(Five hundred years from now, according
To philosophic reckoning),
Our highroads then shall surely be
Improved by us surprisingly.
Then smooth and paved the roads shall run
Through Russia, making all parts one,
And iron bridges huge in size
Shall span the streams. We'll tear to shreds
The mountains, and the river beds
We'll tunnel under, and make rise
At every station on the way
An inn where Christian folk may stay.

34

Our roads are horrible at present,
Our bridges rotten at the best;
The fleas and bedbugs at the stations
Allow us not a minute's rest.
There are no inns. A hovel, cold
And bare of food, displays an old
Pretentious menu thick with stain
To tease the appetite in vain.
Meanwhile before a sluggish fire
Our own uncouth Cyclopes bend
And with their Russian hammers mend
The flimsy products we admire
And get from Europe. And they bless
Our ruts and holes so pitiless.

35
But in the cold of winter weather
The trip is easy and not long;
The roadway is as smooth and pleasant
As verses in a modish song;
The Russian troikas still excel
And our Automedons as well.
The mileposts flashing by are one
Long fence, so quickly do they run.
But Madame Larin traveled still
With her own horses, not by post,
Because she dreaded so the cost
Of hire, so Tanya had her fill
Of crawling through the country ways.
Their journey lasted seven days.

36
But it is nearly done. Before them
The domes of white-stoned Moscow rise,
Her ancient golden crosses lighting
A conflagration in the skies.
My brothers, how I loved to see
That semicircle suddenly
Unroll, of churches, belfries, towers,
Of gardens, palaces, and flowers!
How often, wandering far apart
From you in wretched journeying,
O Moscow, did that echo bring
A sudden passion to my heart!
And for a Russian what profound
Emotion rises with the sound!

37

There Peter's castle rises darkly
Within its grove of trees and boasts
Its latest fame. Here, drunk with conquest,
Napoleon waited with his hosts
To see a Moscow on her knees
Present the ancient Kremlin's keys;—
But all his waiting was in vain:
For never did my Moscow deign
To offer gifts or bow before
The hero, though the day was lost.
No, she prepared a holocaust
For the impatient conqueror;
As he stood there and dreamed, there came
A sudden burst of angry flame.

38

But now goodbye, Petrovsky castle,
You witness of a dead renown!
On, on! The pillars of the gateway
Already whiten; and now down
Tverskaya street and over ruts
And bumps they hurtle. Parks and huts
And palaces go flashing by
And flocks of jackdaws perching high
On crosses, sentry boxes, boys,
Women and merchants, lampposts, sleighs,
Men of Bokhara, balconies,
Gardens and convents, streets and noise,
Apothecaries, Cossacks, shops,
And gates with lions on their tops.

39, 40

Six hours the tiresome journey lasted
And then in Kharitony lane
The coach stopped at the countess' mansion
Who was about to entertain
Her cousins through the winter. Here,
An invalid in the fourth year
Of a consumption now, she lay.
A Kalmuk, spectacled and gray,
Attired in a torn caftan,
A stocking in one hand, threw wide
The door, and from the room inside
The countess stretched on the divan
Called out to them, and in a mist
Of tears the two old cousins kissed.

41

"Countess, *mon ange!*"—"Pachette!"—
   "Alina!"—
"How wonderful!"—"How long it seems!"—
"You'll stay with me?"—"My darling
   cousin!"—
"Sit down! It's like the best of dreams!"—
"It's like a novel coming true!"—
"And I have brought Tatyana, too."—
"Ah, Tanya! Child, come over here!
 Do you remember, cousin dear,
 Your Grandison?"—"Ah, Grandison!
 Yes, I remember perfectly!
 And tell me, cousin, where is he?"—
"In Moscow, at St. Simeon.
 He called on me last Christmas Eve.
 His son's just married, I believe."—

42

"And then that other— But we'll gossip
Some other time. And we must show
Your Tanya here to her relations
Tomorrow. I'm too ill to go
With you, alas! I hardly walk.
But you're too tired now to talk.
Let's go and rest together, for
My strength is gone, my chest is sore.
Not only grief but joy appears
To be a burden, darling, now.
I'm good for nothing, anyhow.
Old age is odious!" So in tears
And growing weaker bit by bit
She ended in a coughing-fit.

43

Her poor aunt's joy, her fond caresses,
Moved Tanya, and yet she, who had
Been used to her own little chamber,
In this new house was always sad.
The silken curtains of her bed
Hung soft above a restless head,
And when at dawn the bells began
To ring and call the laboring man
To work once more, Tatyana rose
And sat beside the window pane.
But when the sun has come again,
No well-known fields—its rays disclose
A narrow yard's circumference
With stables, cook-house, and a fence.

44

Now every day they take Tatyana
To family dinners where they press
On ancient sires and ancient granddames
Her absent-minded listlessness.
For everywhere their kinsfolk greet
The new-come visitors; they meet
The warmest hospitality.
"How Tanya's grown! It seems to me
I stood godmother yesterday!"—
"I held you in my arms, my dear."—
"And I, I used to pull your ear."—
"I gave you gingerbread," they say.
And all the older ladies sigh
In chorus,"How the years go by!"

45

Here all is as it was and nothing
Has changed with them and nothing will:
Here Aunt Elena, the old princess,
Has on the same lace bonnet still.
The same paint on Lukerya Lvovna,
The same lies from Lyubov Petrovna,
Ivan Petrovich the same bore,
Semyon as stingy as before,
Pelagea Nikolayevna
Still has as chief of favorites
Monsieur Finemouche, and the same spitz
And spouse, who holds his club in awe,
Who's just as deaf and calm, and who
Still eats and drinks enough for two.

46

Their daughters first embrace Tatyana
And then these Moscow Graces put
Her to a close examination,
Without a word, from head to foot.
They find her odd—to suit their whim
A bit provincial and too prim,
Too pale and slender for her size,
But quite nice-looking otherwise.
And then, obeying instinct, they
Make friends with her and take her to
Their rooms and squeeze her hand and do
Her hair in curls the latest way
And kiss their cousin and impart
Their girlish secrets of the heart.

47

Their own and others' latest conquests,
Their hopes and dreams and jokes they share
With Tanya in a flood of gossip
Just touched with scandal here and there.
And then they softly ask in turn
If no one makes her spirit burn,
And wait to hear an answering stream.
But Tanya listens in a dream,
Indifferent to all she hears;
She does not understand this art—
And all the passion of her heart,
The sacred pledge of joys and tears,
She guards as she has always done
And will not share with anyone.

48

Tatyana would have liked to listen
And hear society converse,
But in the drawing rooms they babble
Of trivialities or worse;
So apathetic and so pale
Are all, their very scandals fail
To interest. In the arid mass
Of news and gossip she hears pass
About no gleam of wit all day.
Not even at random or by chance
Did one surprise a merry glance,
No joking ever made them gay,
And in that empty world of chaff
No folly that could make one laugh.

49

The groups of youthful officeholders
Who haunt salons would deign to fling
A glance at Tanya and discuss her
In phrases far from flattering.
One melancholy youth does feel
That she embodies his ideal
And, leaning on the doorpost, he
Indites to her an elegy.
And once Prince Vyazemsky sat down
By her in some dull drawing room
And managed to dispel her gloom,
And one old dandy of the town
Then asked her name and even took
The pains to straighten his peruke.

50

But when Melpomene delivers
Her loud, slow-moving eloquence;
When she displays her tinsel trappings
To an indifferent audience;
When friendly clapping cannot keep
Thalia from her tired sleep
And youthful lookers-on will see
And love none but Terpsichore
(Exactly like our own young days),
Then nowhere in the glittering rows
The boxes and the stalls inclose
Do any jealous ladies raise
Lorgnettes to see Tatyana pass,
Nor gallants lift an opera glass.

51

They take her to the Club—a ferment
Of crowds and heat and deafening roar.
The blaring band, the glittering candles,
The couples whirling on the floor,
The fluttering dresses and the sea
Of faces in the gallery,
The brides arranged in a half-moon—
It almost makes Tatyana swoon.
Here, bold and proud, you may perceive
The famous dandies of the day
With their inordinate display
Of vest and eyeglass, and, on leave,
The young hussars who dash in here
To dazzle, charm, and disappear.

52

The night has many stars to charm us,
And Moscow many beauties too,
But brighter than her sky companions
The moon in the transparent blue.
So she to whom I would aspire
But dare not trouble with my lyre
Like that majestic moon once shone
Among all womankind alone.
How proud the heavenly sufferance
With which she moved on earth, and how
Compassionate her breast and brow!
How languid was her lovely glance!
But stop! For you have long since paid
Your frenzied tribute to that maid!

53

Confusion, laughter, bowing, stamping,
Mazurka, waltz, and galop, while
Between two aunts beside a column
Tatyana sits beyond the file
Of dancing-partners, quite unseen.
She hates this world where all careen
And bustle—she is stifled here.
She longs to see the river clear
And flowing where she spent her hours
In country quiet, and the places
She knows—and her poor peasants' faces;
To have her novels and her flowers,
And see the avenue of lime
Where he had talked with her that time.

54

While Tanya wanders so in fancy,
The noisy ballroom all a blur,
A certain general high in station
Has never moved his eyes from her.
The old aunts give a wink apiece
And both together nudge their niece
And whisper,"Quick! Look over there!
Upon your left!"—"What is it? Where?"—
"No matter what, just look! See how
Those officers are talking. They
Have moved and one has turned away.
There, you can see his profile now.
Look quick, before they come between!"—
"That big, fat general, do you mean?"

55

So we felicitate Tatyana
Upon her conquest. Now we bring
Our story back to meet the hero
Whose tale it is we chiefly sing.
And as we pause, a word or two.
I sing a youthful friend, one who
Is all caprices, and I ask
Thy blessing on my lengthy task,
O Epic Muse! Nor let me lack
Thy faithful staff to lean on, and,
To keep me straight, thy guiding hand!
Enough! The burden's off my back,
My debt to classicism paid,
Though late, my introduction made.

Canto EIGHT

Fare thee well, and if for ever,
Still for ever fare thee well.

—BYRON.

1

When in the still Lyceum garden
I flourished many years ago,
I took delight in Apuleius
But did not read my Cicero.
There in dim valleys in the spring
Where cries of swans went echoing,
By waters gleaming silently,
The Muse began to visit me.
My student cell was all ablaze
With sudden light, for there the Muse
Gave banquets; there she would diffuse
Sweet fancies out of childhood days
And glorious visions of the past
And dreams that made the heart beat fast.

2

Then all the world received us fondly
And swift successes winged our stride;
Then old Derzhavin gave his blessing
To our attempts before he died.
And Dmitriev did not censure us
And Russia's stern and vigorous
Protector stopped his work to smile
At our shy Muse a little while.
And you, the ardently inspired,
Who turned all loveliness to art,
The idol of the maiden heart,
Did you not, by your passion fired,
Your hand stretched out to me, proclaim
I, too, should follow shining fame?

3

And I, who always held my passions
To be an all-sufficient guide,
Went off to share my thoughts and feelings,
My young Muse dancing at my side,
To hot debates and feasts and din
On which the watch might well break in.
So to the maddest feasts of all
She brought her gifts, and, like a small
Bacchante, played and sang before
The goblets and the guests, while they,
Those gallants of a bygone day,
Pursued her madly more and more.
And there among that kindly crowd
My thoughtless playmate made me proud.

4

But fortune threw me angry glances
And drove me far. She followed me.
How often on some silent journey
Has her caressing company
Beguiled me with a glamorous
Old tale! Far in the Caucasus
She's galloped with me like Lenore
Past moonlit rocks; and on the shore
Of Taurus by the midnight seas
She often led me by the hand
To hear the crashing ocean and
The whispering Nereides
And the eternal waves whose choir
Extols the Universal Sire.

5
And then my Muse, forgetting banquets
And all the noisy ornaments
Of city life, went off to visit
The wandering tribesmen in their tents
Upon the far Moldavian plains.
There she grew wild and in her strains
Forgot the speech she'd learned among
The gods for this new savage tongue,
And these rude songs now charmed her ear.
Then in my garden suddenly
A young provincial maid—so she
This time had chosen to appear—
With thoughtful, melancholy glance
And in her hands a French romance.

6
But now for the first time I take her,
My Muse, to view society,
And I observe her country freshness
With an uneasy jealousy,
While through the crowd of diplomats,
Of warriors, fops, aristocrats,
And haughty belles she softly slips,
A smile of pleasure on her lips,
And then sits down and watches how
They talk, and hears the flounces swish
And sees the guests come up who wish
To greet their hostess with a bow,
And notes how well the men's dark dress
Frames in the ladies' lustrousness.

7

She likes the oligarchic order
To which their intercourse adheres;
She likes their pride and cold aloofness
And all their varying ranks and years.
But in that chosen company
Who is it stands so gloomily,
A stranger to them all, it seems?
The faces flash and fade like streams
Of tiresome specters, barely seen.
And what does he attempt to hide,
The spleen, or a tormenting pride?
Who is he? Can it be Eugene?
Yes, it is he, no room for doubts—
"How long has he been hereabouts?

8

"Is he the same, or grown more settled?
Must he still always play a part?
What is his latest notion, tell me,
And what new fashion will he start?
What will he be? Melmoth today?
World citizen or Quaker, say?
A patriot, some fanatic soul,
Childe Harold? What is now his rôle?
Or do you think he'll be a nice,
Good fellow, just like everyone,
And leave a fashion we've outrun?
At least, that last is my advice.
The world is tired of his show."—
"Then do you know him?"—"Yes and no."—

9

"Why do you speak with such disfavor
About him? Is it that we all
So love to meddle and to censure?
Or that unfettered spirits call
Forth either rage or mockery
From every vain nonentity?
Or that a freedom-loving mind
Disquiets us, and we're inclined
To take the spoken word for deed?
Or that stupidity is sly
And careless and pomposity
Turns trifles to a solemn creed?
Or do the mediocre seem
The only subject for esteem?"

10

Oh, blest the man whose youth was youthful,
Who ripened with a gradual ease
Through years of growth and learned to suffer
The chill of life by slow degrees;
Who never yielded to absurd
Daydreams, nor shunned the common herd;
At twenty-one a dashing swell,
At thirty married very well,
At fifty with untarnished name
And free from debt, prepared to earn,
All comfortably and in turn,
His share of fortune and of fame;
Whom no one knows as other than
"N. N.—that most distinguished man."

11

But it is sad to think how often
We have betrayed our youth, and how
She also has been false and faithless
And casts us off with nothing now;
That our most high and lofty aims,
Our brightest hopes, our freshest dreams,
Have died in turn until they all
Lie rotting like the leaves in fall.
It's hard to look ahead and see
A string of dinners stretch in sight
And nothing else; to make a rite
Of living, and forever be
With decorous people everywhere
Whose thoughts and views we do not share.

12

Once having been the heated subject
Of talk for men of sense and wit,
One cannot bear to pass among them
For an eccentric hypocrite
Or for a madman sunk in gloom
Or some satanic thing of doom
Or for a demon wild and grim.
Onegin, to return to him
Who'd fought and killed his only friend,
Who'd lived till twenty-six a life
Of idleness,—without a wife,
Without employment, with no end
Ahead, but bored and restless too,—
Had no idea what to do.

13

A helpless discontent possessed him,
A longing for a change of scene,
A feeling few endure with pleasure;
And so he left the lonely green
Of woods and fields, the village lost
In quiet, where a bloody ghost
Appeared before him every day,
And traveled aimlessly away
Wherever chance might choose to call.
But travel, too, like everything
He had attempted, failed to bring
His boredom any help at all.
Now home he came direct from ship
To ball, like Chatsky from his trip.

14

And now a ripple stirred the ballroom,
A whisper running through the hall—
A lady had just entered, followed
By an imposing general.
She was not talkative nor cold
Nor hurried nor yet overbold,
With none of that successful air
That challenges a room to stare;
No little tricks put on for show,
No foolish smile. She seemed to be
In all her calm simplicity
A portrait of the *comme il faut*.—
Shishkov, I beg you tolerate
The phrase: it's one I can't translate.

15

The ladies moved a little nearer;
The older ones all smiled; the men
Bowed just a little lower, hoping
To intercept her glance; and when
The young girls passed her one could see
Them move and speak more quietly;
And straighter, taller for his pride,
The escort moving at her side.
She was not beautiful, and yet
You could not find a single trace
In bearing, figure, dress, or face
Of what the fashionable set
In London circles would have slurred
As *vulgar*—I must use the word.

16

I like it but I can't translate it—
It's new among us, and I am
Not sure that it will find much favor,
Though it would suit an epigram—
But let us watch our lady where
She sits with her unconscious air
Of charm and unaffected grace
Beside a table in the place
Next to Nina Voronsky, she,
The Neva's Cleopatra, who
With all her marble beauty you
Will readily agree with me
Did not outshine her neighbor, though
She was so dazzling bright a show.

17

"It can't be," thinks Onegin, puzzled;
"But she is very like—and yet—
  That village buried in the country!"
  And his ubiquitous lorgnette
  Is lifted, while he tries to find
  The likeness that has brought to mind
  The face that he had known long since.
"Who is the lady yonder, Prince,
  The one in crimson over there
  With the ambassador from Spain?"
  The prince looked at Eugene again—
"You must be introduced to her,
  You've lived too long outside our life."—
"But tell me who she is."—"My wife."—

18

"You're married, then! I didn't know it.
  And how long since?"—"Two years."—
      "To whom?"—
"Her name was Larin."—"Not Tatyana?"—
"You know her?"—"I lived near their
      home."—
"Then come!" In such an unforeseen
  Encounter Tanya met Eugene,
  Her husband's relative and friend.
  She saw him come and slowly bend
  Before her. But although her heart
  Beat wildly with the swift surprise
  Of what was there before her eyes,
  No sign of it did she impart,—
  No, not a token manifest,—
  Her bow was calm and self-possessed.

19

She did not make one startled movement,
She did not flush nor yet turn white,
Her forehead did not twitch or quiver,
She did not press her lips more tight,
And though he looked with all his eyes
Onegin could not recognize
The old Tatyana anywhere.
He would have liked to talk with her
But could not start. She asked him then
How long he'd been there, whence he'd come,
If he'd been in their parts at home;
Then, turning to the prince again,
Fatigued, she glided toward the door
And left Onegin on the floor.

20

How could this be the same Tatyana
Whom he had talked with face to face
At the beginning of our novel
In that remote provincial place,
And in a fit of moral zeal
So nobly lectured for her weal?
Whose letter he still treasured, where
Her heart had laid itself quite bare,
Where all she said was frank and free?
That little girl—or had he dreamed?—
That little girl whom he had deemed
A humble mate for such as he!
Had that same child from whom he'd turned
Become so cool and unconcerned?

21

He left the crowded party sadly
And drove off home. But when at last
He fell asleep a dream disturbed him,
Now dark, now lovely, from the past.
He woke. A letter to invite
Onegin to Prince N's that night
Arrived. "Good God! Her house! Yes, I
Will go!" And a polite reply
Was quickly scribbled off and sent.
What was the matter? Dreams again!
His heart was quivering that had lain
So sluggish and indifferent!
Vexation? Pride? Or, heavens above!
Once more that youthful trouble, love?

22

Again Onegin counts the hours,
He cannot wait for night once more;
The clock strikes ten and off he rushes
And enters at the prince's door.
All tremulous he makes his way
To where Tatyana is, and they
Are quite alone a little. Yet
Onegin finds he cannot get
The words to come. In awkward gloom
He scarcely answers what is said
While in his dazed and whirling head
One stubborn thought alone finds room,
And gloomily he stares, while she
Sits calmly, coolly, quietly.

23

Her husband comes at last. His entrance
Breaks up the awkward *tête-à-tête*,
And with Onegin he rehearses
Old jokes and pranks of ancient date.
They laugh, and other guests come in;
Some grains of malice now begin
To salt the talk, which whirls around
The hostess with the lively sound
Of nonsense sparkling easily.
And then they turn to speak about
More serious subjects, still without
Eternal truths and pedantry,
But sprightly words that one could hear
Without a jarring on the ear.

24

Here were the flower of the city,
The modish and the lordly ones,
The faces one was always meeting,
The necessary simpletons,
The hard-faced ladies growing old
In caps and roses manifold,
The many maidens with no grace,
Of rigorous, unsmiling face,
And an ambassador who spoke
Of government affairs and an
Old gray-haired, perfumed gentleman
Who made his little ancient joke
Quite to the point, upon the whole,
Which nowadays is somehow droll.

25

Here was a gentleman devoted
To epigrams and always vexed—
He didn't like the tea they served him,
Nor the last novel that perplexed
The world, the magazines, the war,
The orders that two sisters bore,
The stupid ladies, boorish men,
The snow, nor his own wife again.
. . . .

And there his daughter you might see,
So hunchbacked, and so slovenly,
So small, with such a piping voice,
That straightway every guest was quite
Convinced she had both wit and spite.

26

And there Saburov was, whose baseness
Of soul had brought him fame, and who,
Saint-Priest, with so much album-drawing
Has dulled your pencil-points for you.
And there another potentate
Of ballrooms stood, a fashion plate,
Pink as Palm Sunday's cherubim,
Tight-laced and mute, with every limb
Immovable. And there you'd see
A traveling young insolent
Whose careful, pompous bearing sent
A smile through all the company,
Who, with an interchange of looks,
Set down their verdict in their books.

27

Throughout the evening all Onegin
Could think of was Tatyana—not
The timid, simple girl who'd loved him
And seemed to suit a humble lot,
But this new princess, worshipful
And goddess-like, unreachable,
Upon the royal Neva's bank.
O mankind, from whatever rank
You come, you're like your Mother Eve:
That which you have you do not prize;
So constantly the serpent tries
To tempt you till you cannot leave
The one forbidden apple there
Without which Paradise is bare.

28

How changed and different is Tatyana,
How quickly it has come to pass!
How skillfully she has adopted
The ways of this restricted class!
For who would think this ruling queen
Of haughty drawing rooms had been
A gentle girl devoid of art!
And yet he used to stir her heart—
She used to grieve for him and lie
Awake and dreaming till the dead
Of night, when Morpheus touched her head,
And watch the moon sail down the sky
And wish that she might humbly spend
Her life beside him till the end.

29

Love has its subjects in all ages,
But to the young its transport yields
An innocent and fruitful pleasure
Like summer showers on the fields.
The rain of passion but renews
Their life, they ripen in its dews,
And from the young and vigorous root
Come fertile bloom and luscious fruit.
But when the years decline and all
The forces fail that once we had,
The marks that passion leaves are sad;
For like the storms of chilly fall
It turns the meadow to a slough
And strips the leaves from off the bough.

30

There is no doubt—Eugene had fallen
In love with Tanya like a child;
He spends his days and nights in visions
And lover's torments hot and wild.
He does not heed the stern reproach
Of reason; every day his coach
Is driven up before her door—
He haunts her footsteps more and more.
He now is glad if he can throw
Her boa round her or so much
As for one instant hotly touch
Her hand or clear her way and show
Her through the liveried ranks, or if
He can pick up her handkerchief.

31

She did not pay the least attention—
He might keep struggling till he died;
She saw him at her house quite freely,
In public distantly replied
To all he said—sometimes a bow,
And sometimes she did not allow
Him even that—for coquetry
Is banned in true society.
Onegin now began to pine—
She did not see or did not care.
He grew quite pale and had the air
Of one approaching a decline.
The doctors sent in their report:
He'd better try a health resort.

32

And yet he stayed, though he was ready
To write his ancestors they soon
Should meet; and still Tatyana, ruthless
Like all her sex, would grant no boon.
But he possessed a stubborn will
And would not yield, but struggled still
And, bolder than a healthy man,
In shaky writing he began
A missive to her, filled with much
Devotion, though he rightly held
Most letters vain; but now there welled
Within his heart a torment such
As could no longer be endured:
Here is his letter, word for word.

ONEGIN'S LETTER TO TATYANA

I know already how offended
You'll be with me when I confess
My wretched secret, and how bitter
A scorn your face will then express.
What do I want from you, and why
Declare you are my all on earth?
To what malicious joy am I
Perhaps this moment giving birth!

We met by accident one day
And when I saw you giving way
To tenderness I did not quite
Believe nor court such sweetness when
I did not wish to lose just then
My freedom, hate it as I might.

And then there rose another bar
In Lensky's sacrifice to fate,
And I was eager to be far
From everything I'd known of late.
I went away. Unknown, unbound,
I thought that freedom might possess
A substitute for happiness;
But I mistook myself, I found.

No, just to see you through the days,
To follow everywhere you go,
To catch sometimes your gentle gaze,
To see your lips, and eyes, and know

*That I can hear you speak, to feel
That nothing in you is amiss,
To faint with pain you will not heal,
To pine and dwindle—all is bliss!*

*But that is what I may not do.
I trail at random everywhere
When days and hours and moments, too,
Are precious and I cannot spare
For idle boredom time that fate
Has shortened. For a heavy weight
Is on me, I am doomed to die,
And all that can prolong my stay
Is knowing when I wake that I
Shall see you sometime in the day—*

*I am afraid that you will see
In this sincere and humble prayer
A despicable strategy
And I once more shall have to bear
Your stern rebuke . . . Oh, if you knew
What tortured longing love can be!
How every hour I burn anew
And reason is no help to me!
And how I long to press your knees,
To weep my love out at your feet,
To speak to you of ecstasies,
To scold and promise and entreat!*

But I must look at you instead
With a pretended calm. Each word
And quiet syllable that's heard
Must sound good humored and well bred!

So be it! It is now too late
To fight against what has to be,
I'm at your mercy utterly
And I surrender to my fate.

* * *

33

No answer came. A second letter,
A third—and no reply to it!
And then one evening at a party
He entered. She was opposite;
But how relentless and how grim!
She would not see nor speak to him.
No, every trace of warmth was lost
As in a January frost.
How stubbornly her face concealed
Her indignation! Searching there
Eugene could see no melting where
A sign of pity was revealed;
Of tearstains not a single mark,
But only anger, cold and dark,

34

And some slight fear that now her husband
And her new world might see unrolled
Her early folly and her weakness
And all Onegin could have told.
Eugene departed hopelessly
And cursing his insanity;
Then in affliction deep and sore
Renounced the futile world once more
And in his silent study, bowed
And bitter, he recalled the days
When hypochondria used to gaze
At him from every noisy crowd
And caught him, rattled every bone,
And locked him in the dark alone.

35

Once more he turned to random reading
And brought out Gibbon and Rousseau,
Chamfort and Herder and Manzoni,
Bichat, Madame de Staël, Tissot.
He read the skeptical Pierre Bayle
And then the works of Fontenelle
And some of our own authors too—
No volume he would not look through:
An almanac, a magazine
Discoursing on morality
In which of late they rail at me,
Though time has been when I have seen
The praises flow from poet's pen—
E sempre bene, gentlemen.

36

What then? Onegin read the pages,
But all his thoughts were far away
While dreams and old desires and longings
Came crowding in a wild array.
Between each stale and printed line
He saw quite other phrases shine
In which his inner soul immersed
Itself with deep and eager thirst.
Here lay the secret galleries
Of love's own pictures of the past,
Chaotic visions darkly massed
And threats and talk and prophecies
And fairy tales, a sparkling whirl
Of life, and letters from a girl.

37

And gradually thoughts and feelings
Slipped farther and still farther back;
Before him his imagination
Dealt out its colored faro pack.
He saw upon the thawing snow
A boy lie motionless as though
Asleep at night, but then instead
A voice that echoed, "He is dead!"
And then he saw old enemies
And cowards, wretched slanderers,
And friends, contemptible as curs,
And sweethearts full of treacheries—
Then, gazing out in revery
On quiet meadows, always she!

38

His dreams had grown so much a habit
Onegin nearly lost his mind
Or almost turned into a poet,
Which, I will own, I'd be inclined
To like, and at that time indeed
He very nearly did succeed
In mastering the mechanism
Of Russian verse through magnetism.
Beside the chimney he would sprawl
Just like a poet, murmuring
First "Benedetta," and then sing
An "Idol mio," letting fall
Upon the ashes quite unseen
A slipper or a magazine.

39

The days flew by until from winter
To spring the seasons had revolved;
Eugene had not become a poet
Nor died, nor had his brain dissolved.
The spring revived him. On one bright
And sparkling day he left his tight-
Shut chambers and their heated air
Kept in by double windows, where
He'd spent the dreary winter like
A hibernating marmot; and
Along the Neva where a band
Of glittering sunbeams seemed to strike
The blue and cracking ice, he dashed,
The mud and thawing snowbanks mashed

40

Beneath his runners. But, you ask me,
Where was he going? You have guessed!
Again he must pursue Tatyana,
Poor lunatic, like one possessed.
He entered like a corpse. No one
In anteroom or hall, and on
He went, till, opening a door,
He saw the princess there before
His eyes, alone and pale, not dressed
For callers, and his passion swelled
To bursting as he saw she held
The letter he had sent and pressed
Her cheek upon her hand and kept
On reading softly as she wept.

41

And who, now watching how she suffered
In silence, would have failed to see
The old Tatyana in the princess,
Poor Tanya as she used to be?
Onegin, driven to complete
Distraction, knelt before her feet.
She started, but no anger stirred
Within her as without a word
She looked at him. She saw his white
Unhappy face and longing eyes
Reproaching her, without surprise
And understood it all aright:
The dreaming simple girl of days
Gone by once more was in her gaze.

42

She did not bid him get up quickly
Nor turn her eyes away nor tear
Her limp hand from his greedy kisses.
What was she dreaming, sitting there?
A long, long pause. Then she awoke,
And quietly at last she spoke:
"Get up! For I must talk without
Reserve to you. I do not doubt,
Onegin, that you still recall
The garden and the avenue
Where fate once brought us, me and you,
And that long sermon you let fall.
I listened to you, still and meek—
Today it is my turn to speak.

43

"Onegin, I was then much younger,—
And better-looking, possibly,—
I loved you, and what was the ending?
How did your heart reply to me?
With sternness only, did it not?
A humble girl's devotion, what
Was new in that to you? Yet how
My blood runs colder even now
When I recall your glance again
And all your chilling lecture! Yet
I do not blame you nor forget
You acted honorably then,
And I can thank you for the part
You chose to play with all my heart.

44

"There in the country far from gossip
And standards based on idle show
I did not please you. For what reason
Must you today pursue me so?
Why have you marked me for your game?
Is it not that I've a name
And riches and because you see
Me move in great society?
Because my husband, wounded in
The wars, is petted by the court
And they would all observe the sport
If such a contest should begin,
So that, if you could drag me down,
You'd gain some scandalous renown?

45

"I'm crying—but if you remember
Your Tanya you must know that I
Would rather hear your bitterest scolding,
Your harshest, chilliest reply
Than this insulting love of yours,
These tears and notes and overtures,
If I had any choice. It seems
You pitied once my girlish dreams;
You could respect the suffering
Of one so young and so untaught.
But now what is it that has brought
You to my feet—how slight a thing!
How, with the mind and heart you have,
Can you be shallow passion's slave?

46

"But all this luxury and glitter,
Onegin, has no lure for me.
My house that is so much the fashion,
My triumphs in society,
What can they give me? Even now
I'd gladly leave this empty show
With its distracting gleam and noise
For our wild garden and the joys
Of my old books—the modest lands
Around our house, and all the scene
In which I saw you first, Eugene,
And for the churchyard where there stands
A cross, and shady branches wave
Their leaves above my nurse's grave.

47

"And happiness was then so near us,
So possible! But now my fate
Is fixed. Perhaps I did unwisely—
My mother begged me not to wait—
She wept and pleaded so and what
Was it to me, to yield or not?
I was so wretched—all was one—
And so I married; it was done.
I beg you, leave me. From my youth
I know beyond a doubt that you
Are proud and honorable, too:
I love you, why conceal the truth?
But I am someone else's wife
And shall be faithful all my life."

48

She left him. As if struck by lightning
Eugene stood mute and motionless,
His heart a tempest of emotions,
All passion, longing, and distress.
Then spurs abruptly on the stair
And Tanya's husband standing there.
Here at a point that well may try
Our hero we shall say goodbye
To him and leave him to his fate.
Goodbye for long, forever! We
Have trailed him, reader, tirelessly;
Hurrah! Let's now congratulate
Ourselves on reaching port. I do
Consider it high time, don't you?

49

Whoever you may be, dear reader,
A friend, a foe, I wish to part
From you in amicable fashion—
Goodbye! I hope with all my heart
That in these careless lines you'll see
What you are looking for: maybe
Just relaxation from your work,
A brilliant scene, a clever quirk
Or boisterous recollections, themes
A journalist may use his wits
Upon and gaily pick to bits,
Or simple pleasure, food for dreams,
Mistakes in grammar from my pen—
May all be here! Goodbye again!

50

Goodbye to you, my strange companion,
And you, my true ideal, too!
My labor, long, but sweet and lively
If trifling, now goodbye! With you
I've tasted all a poet craves—
Oblivion of the stormy waves
Of life, and happy intercourse
With friends. How long, since from her source
In misty dream I first beheld
My young Tatyana with Eugene!
Though I had not as yet foreseen
Each incident that since has swelled
My story, through the magic glass
That tells us what shall come to pass.

51

But now of all the friendly circle
Who heard my early stanzas read,
Some are no longer living, others
Far off, as Sadi somewhere said.
They never saw Eugene complete.
And you on whom I modeled sweet
Tatyana, you have vanished too—
How much fate took in taking you!
Ah, happy he who left the feast
Of life betimes and did not try
To drink the brimming goblet dry,
But with the tale half ended, ceased
To read, and boldly broke away
As I have left Eugene today!

Notes

NOTES

(The numbers in the column at the left refer to stanza and line; those at left of the diagonal to stanza, and those at right of it to line.)

Canto One

Motto	Prince Vyazemsky. A friend and contemporary of Pushkin; a cultivated critic, poet, and satirist.
2/5	*Ruslan and Lyudmila*. Pushkin's first narrative poem, published in 1820.
2/14	Written in exile in Bessarabia.
3/13	The Summer Garden. Formerly the garden of the Summer Palace of Peter the Great; later a public garden, the Hyde Park of Petersburg.
12/10	Faublas. Hero of a novel of Louvet de Couvray, French writer of the second half of the eighteenth century.
13-14/	Wherever a stanza is numbered as more than one, it indicates something deleted by the Russian censor or by Pushkin. The same is true where lines are missing.
15/9	À la Bolivar. Bolivar, the hero of South American independence, apparently affected a high hat with a broad brim.
16/5	Talon. A famous restaurant keeper in Petersburg.
16/6	Kaverin. Popular dandy of the day, to whom Pushkin has elsewhere written joking but affectionate verses.
17/11	*Entrechat*. The leap so often seen in Russian dancing in which the feet are struck or crossed while in the air.
17/13	Moïna. The heroine of *Fingal*, a tragedy by Ozerov, a writer who belonged to the Petersburg French school and wrote in the first decade of the nineteenth century.
18/1	Fonvizin. Famous writer of comedies under Catherine.
18/4	Knyazhnin. Dramatist of the time of Catherine.
18/5	Semyonova. An extremely popular Russian actress, 1786-1849.
18/6	Ozerov. See note on 17/13.
18/8	Katenin. Russian imitator and translator of Corneille and Racine.

[217]

18/10	Shakhovskoy. Prince Shakhovskoy, patron of the theater and writer for the stage in the early nineteenth century.
18/12	Didelot. A famous French ballet master in Petersburg.
20/8	Istomina. A very well-known dancer, who died in 1848.
21/14	See note on 18/12.
25/6	Kaverin. See note on 16/6.
32/9	Elvina. Lednicki, the editor of Belmont's Polish translation of *Eugene Onegin*, says that Pushkin adopted the name Elvina as a convention, that in his lyrics he uses it three times to refer to different people; but that here and in the following stanzas the reference is certainly to Maria Rajevsky, whom Pushkin knew in the Caucasus. She later married Prince Volkonsky, the Decembrist, and is famous for her heroic devotion to her husband in his exile. She is probably Pushkin's model for Tatyana.
33/10	Armida. The enchantress of Tasso's *Jerusalem Delivered*.
35/7	Ochta. A district of Petersburg.
35/13-14	Literally, "The baker in his paper cap Has more than once opened his *vasisdas*." *Vasistas* is a French word meaning hinged window, from the German *Was ist das?*
48/3	The poet. Muravyev, who wrote in the early nineteenth century, and the poem is *To the Goddess of the Neva*.
48/8	The Russian text says literally "from Milyónaya street." But the Russian construction requires the genitive case *Milyónoy*. The nominative form *Milyónaya*, which one would have to use in English, will not fit into an iambic line, so I have been obliged to omit the word in the English translation.
49/2	Brenta. A river flowing into the Adriatic near Venice.
50/3	This stanza was written in Bessarabia.
50/11	Africa. Pushkin was of African origin on his mother's side. His great-grandfather was Hannibal, the son of an Ethiopian king of northern Abyssinia, who had been brought to Constantinople as a hostage and there stolen or bought by the Russian envoy and

	taken to Russia. The boy was a great favorite of Peter the Great, who became his godfather and had him well educated. He later ennobled him and married him to a lady of the court.
57/8	Mountain maid. The heroine of Pushkin's poem, *A Prisoner of the Caucasus*.
57/9	Salhir. A river in the Crimea.

Canto Two

Motto	The point is pretty well lost in translation. Pushkin's exclamation "O Russia" is pronounced in Russian like the Latin *O rus*.
5/11	Red wine. This was apparently offensive as being foreign. A Russian would drink vodka.
35/12	Kvass. A thin sour beer, the national drink of Russia.
37/9	Ochakov decoration. A medal given by Catherine the Great after the capture of Ochakov by Potemkin in 1789.

Canto Three

Motto	Jacques Louis de Malfilâtre, 1733-1767, was a French writer of sentimental lyrics.
5/4	Svyetlana. A ballad by Zhukovsky, named for its heroine Svyetlana, was published in 1812. It is important in Russian literary history as being one of the most popular poems of the romantic movement in Russia, and, though strongly influenced by Bürger's *Lenore*, very nationalistic in its description of Russian superstitions.
9/7	Julie Wolmar. The heroine of Rousseau's *La Nouvelle Héloïse*.
9/8	Malek-Adhel. The hero of a novel by Madame Mathilde Marie Cottin, 1770-1807.
9/8	De Linar. The hero of a novel by Juliane von Krüdener, 1764-1824. Puskin calls the novel by Madame Cottin mediocre, that by the Baroness Krüdener charming.
10/3	Delphine. Heroine of Madame de Staël's novel by that name (1802).

12/8	*The Vampire.* A much read tale of horror wrongly ascribed to Byron.
12/9	Melmoth. *Melmoth the Wanderer* was an enormously popular story of the Irish writer, Charles R. Maturin, 1782-1824.
12/10	*The Corsair.* Byron's Corsair, of course.
12/10	The Wandering Jew. Just whose treatment of the Wandering Jew Pushkin had in mind it is impossible to say, perhaps William Godwin's novel *Saint Leon*, which appeared in 1799.
12/11	Sbogar. *Jean Sbogar*, a novel by Charles Nodier, 1780-1844.
18/7-8	Marriages among peasants when they were hardly more than children were not uncommon in eighteenth-century Russia, though both government and church discouraged them.
27/3	*Good Intentions.* A journal, Pushkin says in a note, once published by Alexander Ismailov, which very seldom appeared on time. The editor, on one occasion, excused himself to his readers for his tardiness by saying that he had gone for a walk on Sunday.
29/8	Bogdanovich. Hippolit Fedorovich Bogdanovich, 1743-1802, a writer of anacreontic lyrics and famous especially for his *Dushenka*, a graceful travesty of the *Psyché* of La Fontaine.
29/13	Parny. Evariste Désiré Desforges Vicomte de Parny, 1753-1814, was a French writer of erotic lyrics who had a strong influence on Pushkin's early writing.
30/1	Singer of banquets. Yevgeny Abramovich Baratynsky, 1800-1844, was one of the most important poets of Pushkin's circle. He was stationed as an officer in Finland from 1820 to 1825, and the wild character of the country inspired several of his finest creations.

Canto Four

Motto	Jacques Necker, 1732-1804, the well-known French statesman, father of Madame de Staël.
3/1-3	Prophetic poet. Nikolay Mikailovich Yazykov, 1803-1846, was a talented Russian poet, a great friend of

	Pushkin. Romantic names for women such as these in line three often appear in his love poems.
30/5	Baratynsky. See note on Canto Three, 30/1.
30/6	Tolstoy. Count Fedor Petrovich Tolstoy, 1783-1873, a famous Russian artist, known especially for his engravings and medallions. He was vice-president of the Petersburg Academy of Arts. His cousin, Nikolai Tolstoy, was the father of Leo Tolstoy; his brother Konstantin was the father of the poet Alexis Tolstoy, 1817-1875.
31/10	Yazykov. See note on Canto Four, 3/1-3.
32/	"This contest between the ode and the elegy can only be understood when one realizes that the classical French literary tendency still had numerous supporters among the older generation of Russian writers in the twenties. The elegy was despised as a 'romantic' form. In the drama they adhered strictly to the famous three unities, and the summit of all poetry was assumed to be the heroic epic, with its wholly conventional apparatus of mythology. The younger generation, who were attempting to make poetical diction approach the language of ordinary intercourse, were severely criticized. It was expected that a poem 'in the high style' should be liberally supplied with words in Church Slavic. The supporters of the old school were under the leadership of Shishkov, 1754-1841, the President of the Academy of Sciences. The younger writers founded the society *Arsamas* in 1815."—Note by Arthur Luther in his edition of the German translation of Pushkin's works.
33/5	The satirist. "This is the poet Ivan Ivanovich Dmitriev, 1760-1837, who in a very witty satire called *Other People's Opinion* makes fun of the scribblers of pathetic odes."—Arthur Luther.
35/3	My old nurse. Arina Rodyonovna, Pushkin's childhood nurse, was later on almost his only companion during the years of his exile at Mikailovskoye from 1824 to 1826. Her stories of Russian folklore are supposed to have aroused Pushkin's interest in fairy tales, so many of which he has retold in verse.

37/9	Gulnare. The heroine of *The Corsair*.
43/10	De Pradt. Dominique Dufour de Pradt, 1759-1837, French diplomat and writer on historical and political subjects.
49/2	Name-day celebration. In tsarist Russia the day of one's patron saint, or name day, was celebrated rather than one's birthday.
50/12	La Fontaine. August La Fontaine, 1758-1831, a German author of more than two hundred novels of domestic life. He was extremely popular in his day in almost all parts of Europe.

Canto Five

Motto	See note on Svyetlana, Canto Three, 5/4.
3/5	Another poet. Prince Vyazemsky. The poem here referred to is *The First Snow*.
3/13-14	You who paid. This is Baratynsky, who in one of his poems describes the Finnish winter.
8/12-14	The first song is an augury of death. The cat song "The tom-cat calls the tabby To sleep behind the stove" foretells marriage.
9/14	Agathon. A typically peasant name, like most Greek names then in use in Russia. No gentleman would have been so called.
10/3	Bath house. All Russian estates had bath houses. As it was not customary to hang on their walls holy pictures such as were placed in all the other rooms of the house, the bath house came to be regarded as a meeting place for spirits, and hence suitable for experiments in magic.
10/11	Lel. The Slavic god of love.
22/12	Martyn Zadeka. Pushkin in a note quotes Fedorov as saying that in Russia books on the interpretations of dreams were sold under the firm name of Martyn Zadeka, a worthy man who never himself wrote anything about dreams or oracles.
23/6	*Malvina*. A novel by Madame Cottin, published in 1801.

23/8   Petriad. Petriads were epic glorifications of Peter the Great written in classical-heroic style. Lomonosov, 1711-1765, "the father of Russian poetry," was the author of one very famous in the eighteenth century, though it was never completed. Another Petriad, in ten cantos and composed by A. Gruzintzev, appeared in 1812.

23/11   Marmontel. Jean François Marmontel, 1723-1799, was a French novelist. His novels were much translated into Russian.

27/4   Tambov. "The province of Tambov is credited with a special reputation for dullness."—George Rapall Noyes, note in *Masterpieces of Russian Drama*, p.153.

32/8   Tsimlyanski wine. A champagne-like wine from the Don.

32/11   Zizi. This was the pet name of Eupraxia Wulff, one of the daughters of Madame Osipova, a neighbor of Pushkin's during his exile at Mikailovskoye. Pushkin was intimate with this family during these years, and fond of Eupraxia, a lively girl of sixteen.

36/8   Bréguet. A watch made by the French horologist Louis Bréguet.

40/4   Albani. Francesco Albani, 1578-1660, an Italian painter of the Bolognese school. His pictures were famous for their minute detail and exquisite finish, and he was fond of painting nymphs and graces. Several of his paintings were in Petersburg.

43/11   *Prisyadka*. The familiar Russian squatting dance, performed almost sitting down.

Canto Six

5/7   Kalmuk horse. A horse of Mongol type common along the Volga. It was small, powerful, and of great endurance and speed.

5/13   Véry's. A restaurant in Paris, famous in the first half of the nineteenth century. It was at first in the Tuileries Gardens, later in the Palais Royal.

24/3   Vesper. Pushkin writes Vesper although he must mean the morning star.

15-16/ These stanzas are found in some later texts, but Pushkin himself omitted them in his own final edition. They are as follows:

15

> Yes, for one knows that jealous rages
> Are really, like the plague, a kind
> Of illness, not black spleen nor ague,
> But a disease that strikes the mind.
> It rages like delirium
> With its own symptoms, from which come
> Hot fevered dreams and lunacy.
> May God have mercy if there be
> A torment waiting anywhere
> More searing than its fatal pain.
> He who has borne it will remain
> Immune to torture though he bare
> His neck beneath the axe or walk
> Upon the nettle's burning stalk.

16

> I will not utter vain reproaches
> And vex the stillness of the grave;
> For you are now no longer living
> Who to my youth and passion gave
> A bitter knowledge and, with this,
> One moment of voluptuous bliss.
> For as they teach a little child
> You taught my tender heart a wild
> Deep woe and stirred and troubled me.
> Your softness made my blood grow hot,
> You kindled love and then you shot
> My young heart through with jealousy.
> But it is over and the shade
> Of those sad days of torment laid.

It seems to me that where stanzas have been found and restored, they usually weaken the poem, and I have left it for the most part as Pushkin published it. Stanzas 15 and 16 are typical.

20/14 Delvig. Baron Anton Delvig, 1798-1831, was a lyric poet and a friend of Pushkin's from Lyceum days.

25/12   Le Page. A famous manufacturer of arms.
44/5, 6, 7   The Russian words for sweetness and youth, *sladost* and *mladost*, are rhymes.

Canto Seven

Motto   Dmitriev. See note on Canto Four, 33/5.
Motto   Baratynsky. See note on Canto Three, 30/1.
Motto   Griboyedov. Alexander Sergeyevich Griboyedov, 1795-1829, was the author of the very famous comedy, a classic of the Russian stage, *Cleverness Brings Grief*.
4/3   Levshin. Pushkin's note says that Levshin was the author of a number of books on farm management.
22/6   Those few novels. Pushkin may here be referring to *Adolphe*, one of the earliest of the psychological novels. Its author was the Frenchman, Benjamin Constant de Rebecque, 1767-1830.
39-40/8   Kalmuk. Tatars were widely employed as house servants in central Russia because they were skillful with their hands and because, being Mohammedans, they did not drink.
49/9   Prince Vyazemsky. See note on Canto I, Motto.
52/   This stanza probably refers to Alexandrina Rimsky-Korsakov, later Princess Vyazemsky.

Canto Eight

2/3   Derzhavin. Derzhavin, 1743-1816, was a writer of the pseudo classical school. He has been called Russia's first poet. At a public examination at the Lyceum in 1815 when Pushkin recited his *Recollections of Tsarskoye Selo*, Derzhavin praised him warmly and saw to it that the poem was published.
2/5   Dmitriev. See note on Canto IV, 33/5.
2/7   Protector. This was Karamzin, 1766-1826, the first writer of importance under Alexander I. His *History of the Russian Dominion* had an enormous effect on Russian prose. On a visit to the Lyceum in 1816 he met and praised Pushkin.
2/9   And you. The reference is to Zhukovsky.

4-5/	The references here are to Pushkin's own poems, *The Prisoner of the Caucasus*, *The Fountain of Bakhchisaray*, *The Gypsies*, and the early part of *Eugene Onegin*.
4/7	Lenore. The heroine of Bürger's romantic ballad.
8/5	Melmoth. See note on Canto Three, 12/9.
13/14	Chatsky. The hero of Griboyedov's *Cleverness Brings Grief*.
14/13	Shishkov. An opponent of Karamzin's, a violent reactionary in the war over the Russian language, in which he upheld the use of old Slavonic words.
16/9	Nina Voronsky. The Countess Elizabeth Voronsky.
25/6	The allusion is to two ladies, Alexandra Osipovna Rosset and Stephanie Radziwill, who were made ladies of the court.
26/1	Saburov. Yakov Nikolayevich Saburov was a Petersburg officer of the Guard with whom Pushkin was at first on friendly terms, but with whom he later quarreled. One of Pushkin's poems which was suppressed by the censor was directed against Saburov.
26/3	Saint-Priest. Count Emanuel de St.-Priest, son of a French émigré, was admired and feared in Petersburg society for his drawings and caricatures.
35/3	Chamfort. A French writer, 1741-1794, author of novels, tragedies, and aphorisms.
35/4	Bichat. The French physician and physiologist and a writer in these fields, 1771-1802.
35/4	Tissot. The Swiss doctor and author, Simon André Tissot, 1728-1797.
35/5	Bayle. Pierre Bayle, 1647-1706, a French freethinker and skeptical philosopher.
35/6	Fontenelle. Bernard de Fontenelle, 1657-1757, French poet and popular philosopher.

www.ingramcontent.com/pod-product-compliance
Lightning Source LLC
Chambersburg PA
CBHW021704230426
43668CB00008B/715